Demons of the Blank Page

Fifteen Obstacles That Keep You From Writing and How to Conquer Them

Roland Merullo

Also by Roland Merullo

Fiction

Leaving Losapas
A Russian Requiem
Revere Beach Boulevard
In Revere, In Those Days
A Little Love Story
Golfing with God
Breakfast with Buddha
American Savior
Fidel's Last Days
The Talk-Funny Girl

Non Fiction

Passion for Golf
Revere Beach Elegy
The Italian Summer: Golf, Food and Family at Lake Como

Praise for Roland Merullo's Work

Leaving Losapas
Dazzling... thoughtful and elegant... lyrical yet tough-minded... beautifully written, quietly brilliant. — Kirkus Reviews

A Russian Requiem
Smoothly written and multifaceted, solidly depicting the isolation and poverty of a city far removed from Moscow and insightfully exploring the psyches of individuals caught in the conflicts between their ideals and their careers. — Publishers Weekly

Revere Beach Boulevard
Merullo invents a world that mirrors our world in all of its mystery... in language so happily inventive and precise and musical, and plots it so masterfully, that you are reluctant to emerge from his literary dream. — Washington Post Book World

Passion for Golf:In Pursuit of the Innermost Game
This accessible guide offers insight into the emotional stumbling blocks that get in the way of improvement and, most importantly, enjoyment of the game. — Publishers Weekly

Revere Beach Elegy: A Memoir of Home and Beyond
Merullo has a knack for rendering emotional complexities, paradoxes, or impasses in a mere turn of the phrase — Chicago Tribune

In Revere, In Those Days
What makes [it] stand out from most other contemporary novels is its graceful prose, its deep and decent characters, and its quiet insistence upon the fundamental dignity of humanity. — Seattle Times

A Little Love Story
There is nothing little about this love story. It is big and heroic and beautiful and tragic... Writing with serene passion and gentle humor, Merullo powerfully reveals both the resiliency and fragility of life and love... It is, quite utterly, grand. — Booklist

Golfing with God

Merullo writes such a graceful, compassionate and fluid prose that you cannot resist the characters' very real struggles and concerns... Do I think Merullo is a fine, perceptive writer who can make you believe just about anything? Absolutely. — Providence Journal

Breakfast with Buddha

Merullo writes with grace and intelligence and knows that even in a novel of ideas it's not the religion that matters, it's the relationship... It's a quiet, meditative, and ultimately joyous trip we're on. — Boston Globe

American Savior

Merullo gently satirizes the media and politics in this thoughtful commentary on the role religion plays in America. This book showcases Merullo's conviction that Jesus' real message about treating others with kindness is being warped by those who believe they alone understand the Messiah. — USA Today

Fidel's Last Days

A fast-paced and highly satisfying spy thriller... Merullo takes readers on a fictional thrill ride filled with so much danger and drama that they won't want it to end. — Boston Globe

The Italian Summer: Golf, Food & Family at Lake Como

This travel memoir delivers unadulterated joy... [Merullo's] account of those idyllic weeks recalls Calvin Trillin in its casual tone, good humor, affable interactions with family, and everyman's love of regional food and wine... A special travel book for a special audience. — Booklist

The Talk-Funny Girl

Merullo not only displays an inventive use of language in creating the Richards' strange dialect but also delivers a triumphant story of one lonely girl's resilience in the face of horrific treatment. — Booklist

AJAR Contemporaries
c/o
PFP, Inc
144 Tenney Street
Georgetown, MA 01833
publisher@pfppublishing.com

AJAR Contemporaries Edition, June 2011

Printed in the United States of America

Merullo, Roland
Demons of the Blank Page / Roland Merullo
First AJAR Contemporaries edition © 2011
ISBN-10 0983677409
ISBN-13 9780983677406

Demons of the Blank Page

"I've always found it easy to write."
Kurt Vonnegut

"Writing is easy. All you do is stare at a blank sheet of paper until drops of blood form on your forehead."
Gene Fowler

Table of Contents

Preface

Preface

During the ten years I taught in college, and the numerous writing conferences and workshops I have been a part of since then, I've heard volumes of advice about the technical aspects of writing. Plot, character, pace, description, dialogue, theme, metaphor, symbolism, and so on. In the conferences especially, there has been a lot of good practical information about finding an agent, attracting a publisher, self-publishing, e-publishing, and marketing a book once it is in print. All this is very good, helpful, and necessary. For high school and college writers, the technical material is useful; for those writing a book or hoping to make a career in the world of words, the practical material can provide a clear understanding of the publishing landscape.

But again and again in those classrooms and workshops, I was struck by the fact that very little was being said about what might be called the emotional or psychological aspects of the writing process. Over the course of thirty years in the profession, thirteen book publications, and several hundred articles, reviews, Op-Ed pieces, travel essays, food essays, personal essays, political analysis, profiles, (even one obituary for the New York Times), and thanks to countless conversations with writers — some famous, some widely published and admired, some struggling to finish a first book or find an agent, and some simply hoping to earn a good grade on a college assignment — I know how critical that interior dimension of the writing life is. In this small book I hope to shed some light on that dimension of the work, not as a psychiatrist or counselor, but as an author, because I am sure that writing success — however that term is defined for the individual writer — always has its roots in the soil of the psychological/emotional world.

When I was teaching at Bennington and Amherst Colleges, and even earlier than that at Berkshire Community College and the Massachusetts College of Liberal Arts, I found myself naturally incorporating this psychological material into my workshops, tutorials, and classes. Little by little, as teachers do, I built up a repertoire of examples from my own experience and others'. I used these examples in what I called "mini-lectures", trying to help people who were struggling in mid-project with writer's block, or with getting started, or, at more advanced levels, in conversations with friends who had successfully published one or more books but now found themselves mired in doubt and confusion. In time I was asked to present this material — first at the Solstice Writers Conference in Boston, and then at other conferences, and at colleges and high schools — in what has come to be called "The Demons Talk". The response to this talk, and my own ongoing day-to-day challenges with the less tangible aspects of writing, convinced me that the demons visit everyone, albeit in different forms and at different points in a career.

After a particularly poignant email exchange with a talented friend who was beset by one of the demons, it occurred to me that it might be helpful to put all this into a small book that could be used by students, writers — and perhaps other creative types — in moments of difficulty.

So I offer these thoughts as the fruit of three decades of good and bad times in the life of letters. There is not much in these pages of a purely technical nature because there are plenty of other helpful books and articles that focus on exercises and stylistic skills. Instead, these chapters deal with the less tangible but, I believe, more important aspects of writing success — whether that success is defined as turning in a paper on time, finishing a first project, finding a good publisher, or making a living with words. I offer it with some confidence, grounded as it is in personal experience over a long period of time. But also with a sense of humility, because like the art of marriage, raising children, playing the piano, or studying karate, there is always more to learn; there are always new obstacles and challenges, and always new triumphs.

Demon One:
Writer's Block

By far the most common and painful demon that assails the writer is the one we have come to call "Writer's Block." This is an opponent that deserves capital letters, at least in its introduction, and one that has, over centuries, caused an enormous amount of misery to creative people and ruined promising careers at all levels. It can afflict writers at the very beginning of their working lives — when they are hoping merely to finish an inaugural poem, short story, or essay — and it can descend, bringing with it a cloud of gloom, upon even the most accomplished authors. A history of A's in English class, a long record of previous publications, a string of large royalty checks, even the mixed blessing of fame — none of these is a defense against this demon. It takes first prize in the Enemy of the Writer category because, unless it is conquered, there is no piece of work that can succeed or fail, nothing to hand in, nothing to reject or criticize, nothing to be proud of, or embarrassed by.

I have dealt with writer's block myself, of course, and have observed it in many, many students, young professional writers, and well published friends. It is as common to writers as the head cold is to humans. After years of watching it wreak havoc on so many talented people, I now see clearly that writer's block always has its roots in a single problem: an excess of self-criticism. Some will disagree, citing the psychological complexity of the inability to create. They will argue that the blockage can also come from depression, from an existential pessimism about art or the market for art, the human condition, from family dysfunction, health concerns, time pressure, dislike of a teacher, envy, mood swings, and so on. Yes, true, at any given time, one or more of those troubles can dampen or drown creativity, but the essence of the problem of writer's block — even in moments of depression or envy — is self-criticism.

Like both my brothers and many of my friends, I am particularly prone to self-criticism. One of my brothers and I sometimes refer to it as our default setting. If we had all A's and one B in a college semester, we think: what was the problem in that B course? If we went two-for-four in a Little League game, we twice failed to do what we should have done. If I have a good round of golf and shoot 79, I could have, and should have, shot 75. If I am a good father to my children on a particular day, that night I will remember moments when I could have been kinder, firmer, or wiser, and those small failures will swell up like dark thunderclouds, casting a shadow over the better hours. Somehow, the negative things we think about ourselves seem truer than the positive.

To a point, that kind of self-criticism is healthy. I

would even go so far as to suggest it is responsible for much of the goodness in the world. Most of us prefer to be around people who are aware of what they are saying and doing — or neglecting to do — who pay attention to, and try to eliminate their flaws, who take into account the way their actions affect others. Surely most of the trouble in the world comes from people who do not have that awareness. But, like any good quality, this one turns sour with excess. Some people are so self-critical, so acutely self-aware, that they are all but paralyzed in both creative and social situations. I had a good friend named Richie who was so concerned about doing the right thing at every moment that he told me he carried on an intense internal debate about whether it was acceptable, when he smoked an occasional cigar, to tap the ashes out the car window instead of using the ash tray. Would those ashes on the asphalt make someone else's life a bit less pleasant? Wasn't it his responsibility to do everything he could to make the world a nicer place? Some of the kindest and most thoughtful people can fall into this mindset, worrying to an impossible degree about being an ideal student, or where and how their clothes were made, their food grown, whether certain words or small decisions will end up, thirty years down the road, causing their children pain.

Writing, with its hundreds of thousands of choices, can be a minefield for the self-critical soul. To complicate matters, many people who choose to write (or act, paint, sing, compose, dance, or sculpt) are sensitive by nature. The source of their creative impulse comes from an openness to experience, a fascination with the workings of the world, a curiosity about the way people relate to each other. This very sensitivity draws them to literature, and it can be of great value in the deep communication that often occurs between writer and reader — that must occur, I would argue, for a written work to be successful. It can make us more observant, better able to feel another's joy, pain, and anxiety, and those are valuable qualities for a writer of either fiction or non-fiction.

But if the sensitivity knob is turned a few degrees too far, if the healthy self-awareness and willingness to be self-critical crosses a certain line, then it can be paralyzing. In scholarly types, this takes the form of what I think of as over-intellectualizing or over thinking. I have a European acquaintance who published two well received novels and then took a job as a university teacher. Most of her teaching involved literature classes, not writing classes, and most of those classes involved a thorough analysis of great works of art. It was her job to find enough to say about these books — and to stimulate her students to find enough to say — in order to fill the hour or hour and a half of classroom time, week after week throughout the term. Classes like that can be wonderful. I still remember listening to Professor Victor Terras when I was a Brown undergraduate. Professor Terras was an internationally respected expert on Dostoevsky, and his brilliant dissections of Dostoevsky's novels attracted students who would otherwise never have taken a literature course. With note cards in hand, he would go through, for example, *Crime and Punishment*, from start to finish. Then he'd go back and work through it again, the following week, from a completely different angle. Then, again, from a third perspective. By the time we were finished reading and talking about the novel, I felt as though I had been given a private tour of Dostoevsky's mind, and this was incredibly helpful to me when, a decade later, I started my own first novel.

But in the case of my European friend, going through books this way made her go over her own sentences with an equally fine-toothed comb as she was writing them. For some writers this works well, giving their language a precision and clarity that makes the whole book sing. But for her it was crippling. Each choice — of word, of sentence, of plot turn, of dialogue — gave rise to nagging questions: couldn't this be better, more sophisticated, more ironic? Won't readers think: this is simple and unoriginal? What will the critics say? They will compare it to my other two books, and say I've made no progress at all. This is not even close to the quality of the books I teach and love to read. She fell into the swamp of comparison — with her own work and with others' — got stuck there, and has not yet emerged.

Like so many aspects of writing, the key here is to strike a workable balance. Sometimes in talks at conferences or in workshops I compare that challenge to a person who goes to a party at which he knows almost no one. It is important in those kinds of social situations — and in any friendship — to be aware of what others are thinking of you: you probably don't want to attend a fancy cocktail party in jeans and workboots; you may want to take a shower beforehand, brush your teeth, refrain from dominating the conversation, or making offensive comments. But if you are overly concerned with others' opinions, you will not be able to say a word, and the unnaturalness of your bearing will make it impossible to enjoy the experience.

Obviously, the art of writing and rewriting involves self-consciousness. And, clearly, self-consciousness has a degree of self-criticism to it. We make judgments on the subject we choose for an important term paper, the words we write to begin a story, the characters who fill our novel, the pacing, the tone, the logical argument. But in order to produce work of quality, or, indeed, any work at all, we have to learn to put a regulator — what machinists call a "governor" — on our self-critical voice. We must keep it in its place. We have to learn to balance it with a healthy degree of self-confidence and even egotism. In order to do that we have to first learn to recognize the self-critical voice, and be able to discern the point where it ceases to be helpful and becomes destructive. For those of us who have made a kind of career of looking at our actions through a negative lens, this can be tremendously difficult. Long-time mental habits are not easy to re-route. But if you find yourself unable to begin a project — class essay, newspaper article, novel — or unable to complete it, try looking for the seed of excess self-criticism in your thoughts.

If the first step in combating this demon is to become

aware of what we are thinking about our own work, then the difficulty inherent in that process is that we are asking the mind to be objective about the mind, asking our thoughts to analyze our thoughts, asking one part of our brain to recognize the flaws in the product of another part. There are a couple of tricks that can help with this. One is to be careful about when we decide to read over our work in progress. For those of us prone to changes in mood — and that's most of us — it's important not to try to lift ourselves out of a depression by sitting down to peruse a chapter of a book or poem that is half-finished. There are times in a day and in a week, and places in the map of our mental wanderings where it is wiser to take a yoga class, hit a golf ball, have a martini or a piece of chocolate cake, roll around on the floor with our young kids, and not look at our work. This ability to assess our own state of mind may take years to develop; it is a kind of wise attention and it is indispensable to the process of becoming consistently productive.

In challenging times, some people also play a game of fantasizing as a way of staying positive. I know a writer who holds imaginary conversations with himself, pretending he is answering a call from Oprah. "Yes, I'd be happy to be on your show, and I'm so pleased you loved the book." Feeling a negative mood coming on, he pictures himself climbing the stage to receive the Nobel or Pulitzer. This is something like the athlete who uses visualization before a skating or gymnastics routine, or before hitting a drive on a difficult golf hole. Like those athletes, this writer is replacing a negative outcome with a positive one, in his thoughts.

Other people identify the overly self-critical voice, and speak to it, sometimes mocking it out loud. "There you are, again, my friend. Yes, you are so right, I am worthless. None of this is any good. No one will ever want to read it. In the unlikely event it is published, the critics will tear it to shreds. Thank you for stopping by, and for your wise commentary."

To combat writer's block, a trick I have used with good success, both in writing novels and shorter pieces, is to compose very quickly, without stopping to look back, without giving criticism a chance to derail me. I started doing this with my third novel, *Revere Beach Boulevard*. On a trip to Italy, Slovenia, and Croatia, I wrote the first draft of that book longhand, on four legal pads, in four weeks. I forced myself not to look over what I had written, not to worry about where the plot was going or if I had wandered down a wrong road. When I returned home and typed out the handwritten work, I had only 240 pages, but there was the whole story, set out from start to finish. I spent another year and a half reworking and expanding it, altering and refining a good deal of what I had written in Europe, and while there were moments of difficulty in that process, I wasn't as tempted to quit as I might otherwise have been. I had a book, after all. The only thing I needed to do was to flesh it out, polish it — and that work is much easier for me than the original composition of a story and creation of characters. I liken it to the difference between pushing a boulder up a long, steep slope, and then rolling it across a flat plateau once the slope has been climbed.

When I'm really stuck, I have also resorted to the old high-school technique of automatic writing. I sit down and force myself to write a couple of pages, going as fast as I can, doing an end run around the thinking and analyzing that usually accompanies the start of a book, the difficult middle section, or the challenge of finding the right ending. I don't worry how bad or good it is. I don't even care about grammar; I just get the words down. Often, this will allow me to tap into the subconscious place where stories come from. When asked how she deals with writer's block, Susan Cheever said, "Writing for a small town newspaper I learned to write even when I didn't want to — even when I didn't have anything to say. I noticed that often the writing that felt the worst turned out to be the best." If you find yourself staring at a blank screen or blank page, set a timer for fifteen minutes, put pen to paper or fingers to keyboard, and then just let go. No judgment, no hesitation, no second-thoughts. What comes out will certainly be flawed, but there will almost always be something of value in the words; you will have secured a beachhead in the battle against writer's block.

Other writers I know keep something inspiring next to their desk — photos of children, posters of famous people they admire, religious icons, pictures of a work of art or a place they've traveled to and loved. I have an odd mix of a signed photo of Rocky Marciano (the only undefeated heavyweight boxing champion, who was famous for not giving up, no matter how bloodied he became), drawings of Chekhov and Dostoevsky, family photos and inspiring relics of various kinds.

Others have a special bookshelf on which they keep their favorite works by other authors, the books that inspired them to try to write in the first place. Reading over just a paragraph of a great piece of literature can sometimes push a person past the obstacle of writer's block and into that happier place where creativity flows more easily.

Another trick in the bag is imagining a single person who is a perfect reader for you, who loves what you write and gets your message exactly, and who is inspired by your words. Imagine that person and write the story, book, term paper or essay just for him or her, hearing their praise as you go. Vonnegut said in an interview that his sister was the person he wrote for. "Every successful creative person creates with an audience of one in mind. That's the secret of artistic unity. Anybody can achieve it, if he or she will make something with only one person in mind."

These things are all crutches, yes, and perhaps they will feel forced or artificial, especially at first. Probably that mocking, self-critical voice will turn its acid commentary upon these techniques, ridiculing them as juvenile, simplistic, or useless. That is simply another of the demon's tricks. Press on. Once you get beyond that first blockage, once you learn to identify and dismiss the demon, there is an excellent chance the words will flow smoothly. Once you cultivate the ability to recognize the excessive self-criticism that lies at the root of your paralysis, you will begin to see it as "just thought" not objective reality.

Because a line of thinking is familiar to you does not mean it is the truth. Because it has been with you a long time, does not mean it is a good friend. Because someone else has a similar thought pattern does not mean it is a helpful one. We all have habitual thoughts that we naturally return to, like rain flowing into streambeds after a sudden storm. Try to reroute those streams in your own mind, in the midst of your own stormy moods. Learn to use the small tricks as keys that open the door to your own creative inner room.

When we were living in southwestern Vermont, I used to like to spend an hour in the Sterling and Francine Clark Art Institute in nearby Williamstown, Massachusetts. Admission was free then, and I always found that standing or sitting in the galleries and studying a Bougereau or Sargent painting for a while made me want to hurry home to my desk. Listening to music or walking in nature does the same thing for some writers. Most successful authors employ tricks like this. At one point, when he thought he'd "dried-up completely", T.S. Eliot resorted to writing poems in French; that got him started again, and some fine poems came out of it, too.

Learning to be productive and successful as a writer is partly a matter of inherent talent, mostly a matter of hard work. But an important, subtle, and often neglected aspect of that work is learning to manage one's interior world, learning how to recognize the source of the writer's block demon and to build up a toolbox of skills with which to combat it. A final suggestion, a last tool in this kit, might be just letting the demon win once in a while. There might be days or even weeks when, for whatever reason or combination of reasons, writing is, in fact, impossible. Learning to be at peace with those temporary failures is as important a skill as learning how to struggle against them.

Demon Two
Having to be Perfect

The essayist and critic Logan Pearsall Smith said that, "The indefatigable pursuit of an unattainable perfection, even though it consists in nothing more than the pounding of an old piano, is what alone gives a meaning to our life on this unavailing star."

That's a nice idea, as long as it isn't carried too far.

Closely aligned with the Chief Demon, (a.k.a. writer's block), is a slightly less common but nevertheless dangerous enemy: perfectionism. This, too, is a habit that starts out in healthy territory but can easily cross the line and become something that is destructive to the creative spirit. My wife, an intelligent and well-educated woman and a good writer, once spent a whole night struggling with a college term paper. In those eleven hours, which took her from dinnertime into the early morning, she wrote three sentences. She wanted everything to be absolutely perfect. If it wasn't perfect, it wasn't going onto the page.

Like almost every other activity I can think of, writing is something that can never be mastered. It is a mistake to believe that Leo Tolstoy or F. Scott Fitzgerald or Emily Bronte attained a plateau of such expertise that they never had to challenge themselves, never had to worry about writing a bad sentence, a bad chapter, or a bad book, never faced the demons. My guess is that they did reach a place of confidence where they knew what they wanted to do and knew they were able to do it. At the same time, I'm sure they were constantly refining, posing new challenges for themselves, working to avoid just playing the same fine notes over and over again, and struggling with the limits of even their vast ability.

That refusal to be satisfied, that continual striving for improvement, is the hallmark of all great students, scholars, artists and athletes. And it has been, in some cases, their downfall. If the trunk of the tree of trouble is self-criticism, then perfectionism is one of its main branches. It is helpful to consider where this attitude might originate.

Obviously, some perfectionists grew up in an environment where they were pressed hard to succeed, at any cost, where criticism replaced encouragement, and the twist of disappointment on the parent's face or in a teacher's voice, was enough to spin them down into an eddy of self-hatred. Those old scars are hard to remove, those reactions hard to change. Three of my sisters-in-law are therapists, and they often see clients, who, decades later, still suffer from this kind of childhood pressure and disdain. Ironically enough, people who were raised in difficult situations frequently turn to art as a means of healing those wounds. In the midst of their creative life, though, they discover that the old hurtful voices are undermining the very activity that was intended to silence them. There are no easy solutions to such deeply entrenched mental troubles. In a later chapter, I will suggest some activities designed to pull out the roots of these noxious weeds and plant something better, but these problems are sometimes so serious, and the solutions sometimes so individual, that professional psychological help is called for. Still, recognizing the problem, and identifying its source, is always a useful first step.

The demon of perfectionism can attack even those artists who grew up in the most loving and supportive families. The issue here is that, for many people, artistic creation begins with what might be called a vision. If you sit down in front of a blank canvas, intent on making a painting, you likely have an image in your mind, however general, of what the finished product will be. This image can be vague and half-formed, but it is, I think, what stimulates us to begin the work. I have even heard people suggest that this first image is an intuition of the Divine or Transcendent, of some pure state that supersedes the limitations of human life. Perhaps that is so. Perhaps that is part of the mystery that not only inspires us to create, but moves us when we read a great novel, see a magnificent film, or watch a brilliant athletic or dramatic performance: we are being given a glimpse of some realm of existence beyond the flawed and troubled everyday world we know. Maybe that is why we are drawn to stare at a beautiful face or a snow covered field or the innocence in a child's eyes.

Let us say, at least, that in sitting down to write a paper, poem, article, story, essay, novel, or non-fiction book, there is a part of us that envisions the finished product as something we can look upon proudly, maybe something that will be praised, that will move or inspire others; maybe even something that will tie us, however briefly, to the ecstasy of artistic success. Even if all we are trying to do is write an excellent analysis of a short story we read in class, or compose a pure thriller that entertains someone on a long airplane flight, as the creative process begins, we imagine a finished product that will do this job of analyzing or entertaining perfectly.

This initial aspect of the creative process is something like becoming infatuated. In those first hours and days of connection to another soul, there is a part of us — even if we are too experienced, too scarred to quite believe it — that envisions a species of unblemished happiness. In time, of course, this happiness becomes mottled. There are good moments and bad, traits we approve of and traits we dislike, lovemaking and arguments, intimacy and isolation. Mature souls can see these things as stages in the relationship — the movement from infatuation, through disappointment, to reconciliation and true love. Less mature souls will be constantly running in search of that impossible perfection they sensed at the start.

This is also true of our relationship to the work we are creating. At the onset of the process there is this hopeful sense that we are about to make something with the shine of perfection to it. Intellectually, we may know that this is impossible, but, still, there is a vision. In my case, I picture the completed novel as a sparkling diamond, perfect in its wholeness and composed of intriguing facets, each of which can be looked at and admired individually. The story will have a marvelous wholeness to it, a balance, a symmetry. Within that whole, each individual part — characters, prose, ideas — will have been beautifully rendered. As soon I actually get into the work, however, as soon as words begin to accumulate on the page, what shows itself is my humanness, my imperfection. Set against my initial hopes, these first ten pages, or first ten chapters, or first ten lines don't match up, just as, set against the thrill and gleam of infatuation, the reality of a longer-term relationship can't possibly compete.

At this point, in the work as in the relationship, we face a choice. We can abandon it in disgust, angry at ourselves for being fooled into thinking the idea was any good, or we can move forward. The people who succeed in finishing a piece of writing (not unlike the people who succeed in maintaining a long relationship) are able to come to terms with this disappointment, with their (and their partner's) imperfection. They are able to see the good parts of the poem, and work to change the less than good, and, usually after a lot of effort, they are able to be satisfied with the imperfect result.

A novel I admire probably above all others is Tolstoy's *Anna Karenina*. I have read it several times, taught it in college, and talked about it with fellow writers who share my admiration. In its scope, plotting, and characterization, its intricacies of suspense and its deep understanding of a variety of human personalities, it is widely recognized as a masterpiece. And yet, any writer I know can go through those pages and find weak spots, sections or lines or bits of dialogue that are clearly at a level less than Tolstoy's best. Various readers might disagree about which lines or sections to include on this lower shelf, but no one is going to see perfection in the novel.

Or perhaps I shouldn't say no one. Perhaps the perfectionist believes that book, or some other, to be perfect, and sees in his or her own work only a pallid reflection, a cheap imitation, a much uglier cousin. What is the point of writing a novel, if it is never going to equal the greatness of *Anna Karenina*? This is the swamp of comparison, a mucky, smelly, dangerous place.

In a strange way, perfectionism can be an attempt at defending oneself against criticism before it is ever offered. The perfectionist wants the professor to read his paper, the editor to read his book of poems, the reviewer to read his novel and gush with praise, and if he senses that this will not be the response, he gives up. If I cannot be the best at the game, he thinks, I don't want to play. If I can't be everything, I must be nothing. It's useful, in such moods, or if you are that type of person by nature, to spend some time pondering the weaknesses and failures of the great ones. Read a critical review of a famous author. Watch any sporting event with an eye toward the small mistakes that inevitably pock every performance. Look at the bloopers section of a famous film on DVD. Check out the biographies of history's great figures. Observe any wonderful forty-year marriage. Flaws, troubles, and errors are everywhere to be found. Trying to avoid them is trying to avoid being human. You are not exempt from the law of imperfection that governs humanity. Probably you knew that already, at least in life. But when you began your novel or essay you thought that maybe this time and in this one area you would somehow transcend that law. What you wrote would match the vision that prompted you to write. That perfection on the page lay latent inside you, or had been carefully honed by decades of reading, by hundreds of writing classes, thousands of hours at your desk. Or perhaps you had a more balanced view of your own abilities, but felt that only perfection afforded you a chance of success in the literary world. Look closely at those thoughts, because therein lies a demon. Like the demon of self-criticism, it is not a matter of killing it entirely, but of being able to keep it in its cage, to turn down the volume of its voice, or to banish it, at least for part of every working day, to a Siberia of the mind. Use the urge for perfection to spur you on, as motivation to rewrite, rework, rethink, but not as reason for quitting or despair. Aim for greatness, of course, but if you write something that is merely the very best you are capable of, be at peace with that.

Demon Three
Overconfidence

Excess of self-confidence is a less common demon, but it carries its own deadly venom. I've encountered it more in beginners and college students than in writers who have put in some years and been through the ups and downs of the publishing life. Still, even there it occasionally rears its particularly unattractive head. It is another strange kind of defense, an attempt to armor oneself against the slings and arrows of criticism. This is a waste of energy, because there is no defense against criticism. Anyone who seriously wants to play this game of writing for an audience has to be prepared to take some hits, to be criticized — fairly and unfairly — to be hurt, even humiliated in the public square. No amount of kindness to others, no amount of hard work, no amount of talent serves as a protective ointment against the sting of criticism. For the creative soul, it is third in line behind death and taxes on the list of unavoidables.

I have met a few writers who are so terrified of imperfection, so fragile in the force of their self-belief, that the only way they can go on is to pretend to themselves that they are stunningly good. Some come straight out and proclaim this; others say it between the lines. In a few

students I have known, this lack of humility has been almost amusing. In older, more accomplished writers it is
wholly unattractive.

Often enough, in writers who have experienced some
success, you can see the inflated balloon of ego carrying
them around the room. Sometimes, others buy into this
act; they may even find it attractive to be associated with
someone who believes himself to be so special. Occasionally, workshop participants, and even professional reviewers and interviewers can be seduced by an artist's belief in
his or her own specialness. Writers of this ilk can often be
heard speaking about their efforts in exaggerated or dramatic terms, calling the work they do "torturous" or "bru-
tal labor". In my opinion, people who toil in the fields of
language should use words with more care. Yes, writing
can be difficult. And yes, it is a particular kind of difficulty, different from those faced by a carpenter, taxi driver, or
nurse. But it is not torture, there are harder things in life,
and your success, while it may have come from years of
effort and a large or rare helping of natural talent, does not
really entitle you to claim membership in a higher category
of the human family.

Chances are good that if you are reading a book like
this you are not one of the self-proclaimed chosen few
whose work is beyond reproach — at least in their own
eyes. But it is helpful to understand the illness so that you
can identify and dismiss it when you encounter it, in yourself or in others. The Supremely Confident One hands
you his work to read as if he is doing you the kindest of

favors (in fact, a writer should always ask someone to read his or her work with a sense of humility; you are asking for this person's time, and are often putting the reader in the awkward position of having to tell you, to your face, what he or she thinks of your efforts). Once you have finished, he seems to have an ear only for praise. "Yes, yes, I knew that part was good." Any suggestions or negative remarks are either ignored entirely or met with stiff resistance. Sometimes this resistance is disguised as false openness, "Oh, did you really think that?" Or artificial acceptance: an insincere, "I'll look at that section again." Other times it leads to an argument, with the writer working to convince you of the high quality of the piece, even going so far as to suggest that you misread it, that you aren't literate or sophisticated or intelligent or spiritual enough, you've missed the whole point, and so on.

While it can sometimes be true that a careful reader misses the point, I think it's best to hold to the rule of never defending your work once it has been read. This can be tremendously frustrating, especially in the case of bad or careless reviews, or less-than-thoughtful first responses. As Truman Capote said, "I have had, and continue to receive, my full share of abuse, some of it extremely personal, but it doesn't faze me anymore. I can read the most outrageous libel about myself and never skip a pulse-beat. And in this connection there is one piece of advice I strongly urge: never demean yourself by talking back to a critic, never. Write those letters to the editor in your head, but don't put them on tape."

Trying to convince a reader that she should like what you have written is like trying to convince her that she should like your home-made pistachio ice cream. Make the ice cream from your original recipe. Scoop it into a dish. Hand her a spoon. Watch her face as she swallows, but never try to convince her that she likes what she does not.

If you are one of those people who truly thinks your work is beyond criticism, perfect as written (and sometimes in the first draft) then you need either a serious attitude adjustment or you need to work in complete isolation and never show your work to a lesser soul. It is perfectly fine for you to have faith in your work, to believe it is important and good, to believe in your talent. In fact, it is essential. At some point, now or in the future, you are going to be asking a reader or many readers to devote a few minutes or a few days to what you have written. There is a good measure of ego involved in doing something like that. The problems arise only when that ego inflates to the point where it fills the room, leaving no space for imperfection, no allowance for criticism, no possibility that there is an intelligent reader on earth who just doesn't adore what you have done.

If you encounter this attitude in a fellow writer — in a workshop, say — it is best to offer your response once, straightforwardly but humbly, and not insist on it. You can tell by the intensity of the resistance you meet how open the writer is to suggestions about his work. When the writer argues, gets upset, tries hard to convince you that you are wrong and the work is fine just the way it is, the best path is silence. Chances are excellent that this kind of person will not succeed outside the small circle of his own thoughts, but let the laws of the literary workplace take care of that.

If you recognize this attitude in yourself, picture it as the booster rocket of a spaceship: you need a measure of that conceit in order to push you out of earth's gravity, in order to believe you have something to say, something to add to the already enormous canon of great writing, or merely something that will please your teacher. But once it has gotten you off the ground, cast it away. You are in orbit now. The gravity of earth — your human imperfection — is not holding you, but swinging you in a happy circle. Let the burned-up old shell of overconfidence fall back into the ocean with a splash, and sink to the bottom. And, for the sake of your teacher, friends, acquaintances, and your own writing career, let it remain there.

Demon Four
Choosing the Wrong Reader

Once you step out of the small, secret room of your own creativity — a joyful or a tormented place, depending upon the individual — there always comes a point where you ask someone to read your work and give you an honest response. This person can be a friend, classmate, roommate, or a professional editor, and this moment is always a delicate one, something that has been a source of trouble for many of the writers I have met.

The important thing to remember at this point in the creative process is that readers cover a spectrum as wide as human taste, a band of particularity that wraps around all twenty-four of the earth's time zones.

For potential book authors, it might be wise to keep in mind that those who love, say, the later work of James Joyce, are probably not going to be fans of best-selling romance novelists (though there are a few readers whose tastes are that eclectic.). The person who steps into a bookstore and immediately heads for the engineering section, might not glance at the poetry aisle, and vice versa. The teacher or professor who keeps saying she likes things to be concise, is not going to approve of your work if you indulge your lyrical side and pass in a paper twice as long as it should be. While it is important for students to pay careful attention to a teacher's requirements and preferences, one of the great mistakes a writer of any level can make is trying to please every reader, every time. Even the most successful novelist — let us take J.K. Rowling as a good modern example — is going to leave at least a few readers out in the cold.

So the first thing to consider when choosing a reader is not, how close is this person to me, but what kinds of books or articles does he read? Your roommate reads only fashion magazines and you are asking her to comment intelligently on your haikus. Your best friend brags about not having read a book since college, and you hand him your thousand-page manuscript, hoping for a helpful response. If you have written a police procedural and your mate is a passionate reader of Virginia Woolf, then things might work out all right but more likely you are setting yourself up for an unenthusiastic response. The Woolf fan hasn't read any other detective books, isn't interested in that kind of writing, doesn't like it, doesn't care about it. So he is not your ideal choice, especially when you are starting out and the tender shoot of your writing hopes has just now poked its green nose up into the cool spring air. This bears repeating: The depth of the friendship, marriage, or love relationship should not come into play when choosing a reader, and it can be an enormous mistake to confuse the quality of the personal relationship with the desirability of the reader. Naturally, we care about our writing, and so our first instinct is to show it to someone close to us. But, as the Italians warn you before crossing a street in Rome, *Attenta!* Careful!

I have seen a number of cases where choosing the wrong reader has damaged friendships, even marriages, and other times when it has caused a deep wound in the writing muscle. This happens in school settings, but it is more common among the older set, writers I meet in workshops. Whenever I mention that it might not be a wise idea to choose one's spouse as a first or primary reader, I am aware of heads nodding all around the room. You can almost see the arguments and hurt feelings that have resulted from asking the wrong person to tell you what he thinks of your story. In some cases, like those examples cited above, this is because the spouse or best friend loves different kinds of books than the one you are trying to write... or, doesn't love books at all. In other cases the reasons are more complicated.

For many of us, there is a way in which we look to relationships for stability. In a world of unnerving unpredictability, where good fortune or good health can be lost in an instant, a true friend or a soul-mate is a thick-walled building in which we can seek shelter when the hurricane comes ashore. How wonderful that is. And yet, we have to look at it from the other side of the equation: our friend or our mate may look to us for shelter, too. He or she depends on us to be the person we have always been, to be "there for me" to use a cliché I despise. If that person is a great field-hockey player and teammate of yours, and decides she suddenly wants to quit the sport and devote herself to essay writing, or if your mate decides, in mid-life, that he suddenly is tired of playing the role of dependable businessman who comes home and watches game shows after dinner, and now he wants to hole up in the study and write poetry, that can be threatening. If you have always been the cheerful, outgoing wife who likes to go bowling on Friday nights, or out to a raucous party, and suddenly, age 38, you tell your beloved that you have decided to stay home on Fridays to put in a few hours on your novel. . . well, there are some beloveds for whom that is not good news.

This doesn't have to involve marriage. I have seen the same dynamic at work even in friendships among adolescents and twenty-somethings. Your friend wants you to be the person you have always been. Your admission that you are now writing a romance, a spy novel, or pursuing a career as a writer of food essays, as much as the friend might like to read or eat, can be threatening to varying degrees.

Is this a good person to whom to show your work?

More complicated, still, what if this friend or this mate has unfulfilled artistic aspirations of his own? He has never been able to make the necessary sacrifices to pursue these dreams, he doesn't have the discipline to set aside time and do the work, he can't turn down the volume on his self-criticism, he can't deal with criticism from others, he won't do anything unless he does it perfectly, and so he's afraid to even try out for that play even though his mother always told him he could be a great actor. . . .What kinds of feelings are going to arise in this friend when you make your announcement that you are trying with all your might to win a short-story contest, or going away to a cabin in Saskatchewan for a month to finish your first novel? What is the likely outcome when you ask him to read your work?

I had an experience like this relatively early in my writing life. By that point, I had been at it for seven or eight years, with little success — nothing more than a few small articles published in a local newspaper supplement and one essay in a philosophical magazine. But I had been doggedly working on a book for those years, first in non-fiction form and then as a novel. My wife and I had a friend visiting, and this friend had a huge talent as a painter. But, for whatever reason — lack of self-belief, an excess of self-criticism, an inability to manage time — she had not produced a single painting since college. Knowing of her artistic inclinations, and valuing her friendship and intelligence, I made the mistake of asking her to read a first chapter of the novel I was hard at work on. I might even have compounded the mistake by reading it aloud (something I learned to avoid shortly thereafter; some writers do this, but you are really putting people on the spot if you read aloud to them.) I don't recall. But I do recall her response, which was delivered without inflection and took all of about ten seconds. It was not very good, she said. There was nothing in it that interested or moved her. A bit eager in those early days for some kind of support, I asked her a couple of leading questions with the same result. No interest. No good word. Zero.

It stung, naturally. It planted some small seeds of doubt, too. It wasn't the criticism; it was the complete lack of acknowledgment that there was anything at all worthwhile in my work. The chapter eventually ended up in my first novel, *Leaving Losapas*, which Houghton Mifflin published a few years later with some success, so I must have been able to file her negative response in a safe place. Unfortunately, talented though she is, our friend has never been able to paint anything in her adult life. The lesson was a valuable one, and I've remembered it ever since.

Jealousy is a natural part of the writing life. I think all writers feel it. Some of us struggle against that natural reflex, and others indulge it. In a profession where there are no measurable standards of quality (unlike carpentry, for example, where you can set a level up against a wall and see that you have built it plumb, use a framing square to tell that you have made the corners well, see the building inspector's signature on your permit to know that the structure is safe), it is easy to be unsure about the quality of what you produce, easy to feel depressed if you cannot work while someone else is putting out a book a year, and easy to feel that another writer has gotten praise, fame, and money that you deserve. I'll get into these feelings a bit more in a coming chapter, but the importance of them here has to do with choosing a reader (and being a reader for someone else.) However unlikely it may seem to you, be aware of the possibility that your artistic efforts might make those closest to you uncomfortable. Might. Many good friends are large enough to overcome this. Just be aware of the possibility.

It is important, especially in the early going, to have a reader or readers who support you. What you want in the formative stages of your career is positive feedback, even if it is speckled with helpful criticism. Writing groups can be useful in this regard: often in these settings, everyone is in the same boat and your fellow writers can be supportive and kind.

Later on, (or right from the start if you are a particularly confident person) once you have your feet firmly under you, what you look for is less praise and more suggestion. Again, it is helpful to find a person who likes to read the kind of things you like to write, someone whose intelligence and judgment you trust, someone who can be completely straightforward, but in a wise, not a hurtful way.

There should be no guilt involved in choosing not to show your work to the people you love most. You might need to have a conversation with your husband, explaining diplomatically why you want Paul in the writers' group to read your story before he does — or instead of him — but you have to exercise good judgment. Render unto your friendship what the friendship needs, but give your writing what it needs as well. This sometimes results in a period of argument and strained feeling, but I have found that most friends and spouses, if they really care for you, soon understand how much this passion for writing means in your life, and are willing to make the necessary adjustments.

The last thing I want to say on the subject of readers is: don't have too many. During the writing of my second novel, *A Russian Requiem*, still suffused with the great thrill of publication and wanting to make a careful second step up the literary ladder, I made the mistake of asking thirteen different people to read the manuscript. These were generous friends. They read the long book and offered detailed criticism. The problem was that, even though they all fell roughly into the same section of the reading spectrum and the audience I was aiming at, their responses varied so widely it confused more than helped me. One person would write to say, "I loved it. Great book. The only place I really felt it sagged was in Chapter 31. You really need to work on that." And another would tell me, "Chapter 31 was just brilliant. Can you bring the rest of the novel up to that level?"

Now I have settled on a pattern of not showing early drafts to anyone. A bit farther along in the process — once I feel like I've gotten a manuscript to the point where it is readable, and I can't immediately see what else I might do to improve it — I ask my wife Amanda to read what I have written. Unfailingly generous with her time, an avid reader, she focuses more on the story than the beauty of a phrase, more on whether or not the fictional world makes sense than on any decorations of idea or metaphor hiding in the lines. That is exactly what I need at that point in the process. I can tell by the pace at which she finishes the manuscript whether or not I am in good shape. If she puts it away for stretches of time, or doesn't get all the way to the end, then I know there is a problem. If she goes quickly through the pages scribbling comments in the margin, I know I have achieved at least the first goal: keeping the reader involved.

Later, I will often ask a friend or two, and then my agent for an opinion on a more polished draft. Only then will it go to the editor, at which point I'll get more feedback and do more work.

Learning to choose the people you want — and don't want — to read your work in progress is one of the most valuable skills a writer can develop. While your choice of readers may change over time, the importance of asking the right people does not. Beginning writers are usually more vulnerable, more easily shaken. But writers farther along in their careers often have more at stake — a reputation, a career, a paycheck. Very few writers produce a book without help, and most of us are grateful to those who take the time to go through the work and offer suggestions. Before you ask that favor of someone, however, before you take that first large step into the world of criticism, give careful thought to which sets of eyes you want on your pages.

Demon Five

Choosing (or Never Finding) a Mentor

Some writers damage their work routine by worrying too much about finding the right mentor, or living without one. This is another waste of energy: I know of many authors who have succeeded mostly in solitude, or with the help of a circle of friends that are all equally helpful. In some cases, the beginning or experienced writer is fortunate enough to have a true mentor, one person who helps guide him through the minefield of demons. For some, this person is a teacher in high school or college, or, years after formal education is finished, in a conference or low-residency writing program. For others it is a trusted, well-read friend, sibling, spouse, agent or editor. It is possible, I suppose, to go out looking for a mentor in something like the same way that it is possible to go out looking for a husband, wife, or spiritual teacher. But, as with those examples, it seems to me that there is an element of fate involved: in some mysterious fashion the mentor is also looking for you. If you happen not to meet in this life, don't be worn down by the demon of worry.

When I finally decided, at age 25, that what I really wanted to do was write for a living, I was not exactly at the high point of my life. I had just returned from an abbreviated stint in the Peace Corps, on a tiny, isolated atoll in Micronesia. Physically sick, disappointed in myself for not having fulfilled my two-year commitment, without any health insurance or any money in the bank, I was just unhappy enough to be able to shed everyone else's expectation of what I should do for a career and admit that I wanted to write. This was difficult, in part, because I had grown up in a place where there were no writers. No one I knew, none of my parents' many friends and none of my own, wrote books for a living. None of them worked at a newspaper or magazine. I was aware, of course, that someone did those jobs, but there was an unreal quality to those figures; they seemed almost mythical.

My parents were first-generation Americans and, while they lived good, solid working-class lives, they had never been able to fully use their abilities. Some of their frustrated ambition was transferred onto the shoulders of their oldest child, and so all through high school and college and for the years immediately after graduate school, I carried a heavy weight of those typical American dreams — that I should become a doctor, a pharmacist, a professor, careers that offered prestige, money, security. It took a stretch of travel and exotic jobs — driving across the country, working in the USSR for the US Government, serving in the Peace Corps — and a good dose of hardship — tough, low-paying jobs like parking cars at night in a garage, loneliness, a broken back, a couple of persistent tropical infections, the return to Boston broke, sick, and

— in my own mind at least — a failure — for me to give an honest answer to the question: what do you want to do with the rest of your life?

I started to write. Living in a less-than-glamorous apartment with my more-than-wonderful girlfriend (now my wife of thirty years), and driving a Checker cab three days a week from four in the morning until four or five in the afternoon (for an average salary of two dollars an hour), I spent my free days in the Allston branch of the Boston Public Library with a *Bic* pen and a pad of lined paper, working on a non-fiction book about Micronesia. For money, I drove the cab — which I liked — did temp work in offices — which I hated — made phone calls at night as a paid fundraiser for St. Jude Children's Hospital.

In most of my free hours I wrote.

The next fall, when Amanda found a teaching job on Martha's Vineyard, we rented a small house there at the off-season rates and I went to work for local carpenters, trying to learn a trade for which, in the early years, at least, I showed little aptitude. Though we could have used the money from another full-time salary, I again chose to work only three days a week and I spent the rest of the time with paper and pen, trying to get something — anything, published in a magazine or newspaper. The book I'd started in Boston was going nowhere, unless hundreds of unread handwritten pages counts as somewhere, and I was collecting an impressively long list of rejections on smaller projects. But what I might have lacked in talent and so-phistication I tried to make up for in stubbornness (a pattern that has continued all through my writing life.) In May of that year I had my first acceptance, an essay on solitude for the philosophical journal *Rosicrucian Digest*. I still remember opening the envelope outside the Oak Bluffs Post Office, and finding a check there, for $72.00, and the letter of acceptance. As far as I was concerned, it might have been a Guggenheim.

When high season came and we could no longer afford to live on Martha's Vineyard, we took all our meager savings, bought 10-speed bicycles and panniers, and made a 1000-mile bike trip around New England. That fall, we moved to the northwestern corner of Massachusetts — we did not have jobs there; we simply liked the look of the land. Amanda found work waitressing, then bartending, and I painstakingly built a carpentry career, starting out riding to jobs on a ten-speed bicycle, replacing panes of broken glass and nailing up shingles, and then, mistake by mistake, learning how to cut stair stringers, install doors and windows, build decks. The country was suffering through a recession, work was scarce. We did not have a car at first, or furniture, but we were in love and happy much of the time, and I kept on with the writing, hunched over my yellow legal pads in the Williams College Library while Amanda made pina coladas and poured beer a few blocks away.

Things very slowly improved. She turned her photography hobby into a job at the aforementioned Sterling and Francine Clark Art Institute. I bought a used Sears van and took on larger jobs — painting a two-story Victorian, building a garage. With the help of a first-time-buyer's program, we purchased a four-room house two miles down a dirt road, just over the border in southern Vermont. By this time, in a fit of discouragement, I had thrown away the hundreds of pages I'd written about my time in Micronesia and was working on stories and poems, pitching articles, recording every rejection in a blue notebook. At night, after a day of carpentry and then dinner with Amanda, I'd go down into a corner of the unfinished basement and work at a makeshift desk there — articles, essays, bad poems — and only my own determination, and Amanda's belief in me kept me going. One night the phone rang and the woman on the line said she was an editor from *Newsweek*. At first, I thought it was a friend playing a bad practical joke. But then she told me they wanted to publish an essay I'd sent them and would pay $1,000 — more than a month's pay in those days.

Also about this time — it was 1984 and I had been writing seriously for five years — a man from nearby Williamstown, Massachusetts, called, responding to my ad in the local newspaper. He had some small carpentry jobs he needed done around his house, was I interested? The man sounded grumpy and particular, and if I hadn't needed the money so badly I might have told him I didn't want the job, was too busy, already booked.

But the next day I stopped by, and this man, Michael Miller was his name, turned out to be much more pleasant in person than over the phone line. He and his wife Mary had a new child, and an elderly relative living with them.

The jobs they needed done were within range of my skills: a set of two steps for the back entrance; a railing for the interior stairway. We scheduled a time for the following week and I showed up, unloaded my tools, and started work. While I was nailing together the back steps, Michael came outside and struck up a conversation. For some reason, though I had made it a policy never to use the word "writer" in describing myself (I felt that, until I actually published a book, it would be presumptuous), and though I almost never spoke about my secret dreams with anyone other than Amanda, I must have mentioned my passion to Michael. I don't remember how this came about. Maybe I asked him what he did for work and he told me about his poems and plays. Maybe we started off admitting to each other that we loved to read.

I don't recall, precisely. But after that conversation, after the jobs at his house were complete, we started to get together once a week for coffee or a beer or a pizza and talk about writing. In some ways our histories were markedly different. He was twelve years older, a product of New York City, had enlisted in the Marine Corps instead of going to college and was completely self-taught. He'd gotten married at forty; I had two college degrees and had been married by twenty-six. He was from a Jewish family and I'd been raised a devout Catholic. But a love of books united us, a drive to be creative, and we'd both grown up in rough and tumble neighborhoods with sports and friends and street adventures, and acquaintances who'd gone to jail.

At the time, I did not realize the full extent of Michael's generosity. We met every week for years. He would read whatever I asked him to — poems, essays, short stories, scraps of articles — and offer his criticism with a supportive straightforwardness that would be a model for any mentor. He'd recommend books, poems, biographies of writers, films. When I worried aloud about being thirty-something and unpublished, he encouraged me with anecdotes about famous authors who hadn't published a book until they were forty, or fifty, or sixty-five.

The breadth of his knowledge of literature would have been remarkable for someone with a PhD in the subject. For a person with a high school education, someone who'd spent his life surrounded by people who did not read at all, it was astonishing.

After a year or so of these meetings — I still had nothing to show for my work beyond the *Newsweek* essay — Michael and I had a beer in the bar of the Williams Inn in Williamstown. By this point we knew a good deal about each other's upbringing, and he had a keen understanding of the frustration I felt at my lack of success. It was a mild night. I vividly remember walking out of the building — he was headed home, on foot; I was walking to my truck — and Michael saying, "You should write a novel about the way you grew up."

"A novel!" I replied. "I can't even get a short story published. Other than the Newsweek essay, I can't even get something taken in a newspaper or a magazine, how am I going to publish a novel?"

"Some people are sprinters," he said. "And some people are long-distance runners. Maybe you're a long-distance runner, maybe that's the problem."

Since that spring evening, I have thought about those words hundreds of times. That one sentence helped me more than anything anyone has said to me in thirty years of writing, more than any book I've read or any piece of advice from editor or agent. Maybe by accident, maybe out of some wise intuition, Michael had hit upon a keystone of writing success: while there are some authors, like the late John Updike, who can excel in a wide variety of genres, most of us have one area of natural strength. For another favorite of mine, Andre Dubus, it was the novella. For Isaac Babel, it was the very short story. For Edward Hoagland and James Baldwin it is/ was primarily essays, for Anna Akhmatova it was poetry. It's fine, in the early going, to probe the vast seas of literary possibility, trying your hand at poems, essays, stories, a long work of fiction or non-fiction. And there will always be some people who find success in more than one area. For many, though, the advice from the Tao Te Ching will apply: Take hold of this/Let go of that. The temptation to begin, then abandon, a series of pieces of work is just another sly demon, as is the temptation to work hard at poetry for a year, and, finding no success, switch to essays, then to novels, then to non-fiction, plays, opinion pieces. At some point in the building of a career — this is not true for every writer, but I believe it to be true for most — it is wise to focus your energies in one genre, to work on your sprinting or long-distance running, and not confuse your body by training for both. It might be wiser to diversify only after you've had success in one arena, like Steve Martin playing the banjo, or Meryl Streep singing, or Sinatra going into films.

For me, the change of focus to the novel, while it did not have instantaneous results, marked a crucial turning point in my pursuit of the writing life. Now, twenty-five years after that beer at the Williams Inn, I have published essays, reviews, Op-Ed pieces, travel articles, a couple of non-fiction books, two serialized novellas, and even two short stories in golf magazines (both of which expanded and expanded, threatening to burst out of their genre, and were contained there only by the length requirements imposed by an editor), but it is clear to me that I am most comfortable with the long-distance running: writing books.

That conversation occurred in 1984. As I remember it, I started work on a novel the next night. Six and a half years later it was published. Michael read it in several drafts, week by week, chapter by chapter, sometimes crossing out whole pages and scrawling an angry epithet in the margins; other times he'd bracket long sections and splash lavish praise onto the page beside them. While he could be blunt in his suggestions, they were always thoughtful, and in our conversations he was unfailingly optimistic and encouraging, citing the achievements of people he knew personally, their healthy advances and film options, the way persistence had paid off for them after years of failure and work. His words carried extra weight for me, not only because of our shared passion for literature and the similarities in our upbringing, but because he was compiling an impressive list of poetry publications himself, in places like *The American Scholar* and *The Southern Review*, the kind of acknowledgment I could only dream about at that point. These would eventually lead to the winning of a prestigious prize and the publication of a collection of his poems.

Our friendship went through stages, some of them difficult. At first, I listened carefully to his criticism and suggestions, and had some success — the publication of my first novel with Houghton Mifflin. Michael and I endured a period of readjustment then: he'd still read my work, and I'd still listen, but he was not the only, or even the primary voice in my ear; we argued, went some time without speaking to each other. Later, after I'd had several more books published, and he'd won the prize, we became close again and formed a more mature, more equal relationship, a kind of fraternal partnership in which we still met for breakfast or lunch almost every week and talked about the trials of the publishing world and the challenges of creativity. He showed me his poems and appreciated my thoughts on them. And I still took advantage of his generosity, asking him to read chapters, to comment on ideas I had, to make plot suggestions, to warn me away from the shoals of cliché and inauthenticity. What I valued most of all was his almost unshakeable optimism. In a business full of uncertainty and riddled with failure, that voice was, for many years, a tone I listened to in my hardest hours.

Our friendship hit a weak spot again just as both of us were enjoying some success. I showed him a novel in progress. He critiqued it in a way that bothered me. I felt he was trying to take me back to the old days when I didn't really know what I was trying to do. No doubt, he thought I was being overly sensitive. Maybe jealousy played a role on both sides, maybe it was pride; maybe the friendship, so important to me at one time, and, I think, so meaningful to us both, had simply run its course.

Other friends have helped me along the way, in relationships not as intense but longer-lasting. After I had back surgery in 1987 and couldn't do carpentry work for some months, Peter Grudin (someone else I met through carpentry; I built a large addition onto his Vermont farmhouse) lent me his only computer and taught me how to use it. He, too, has been generous in reading my manuscripts and offering advice. The well-known novelist Craig Nova is a close friend who has read drafts for me, and done a thousand other favors. We email several times a week and talk regularly on the phone, helping each other stay afloat in the turbulent waters of the twenty-first century publishing world. Dean Crawford, a professor at Vassar and author of two books, has been equally kind with his time, reading drafts and talking about the writing process. He introduced me to his agent, who sold my first novel. Jeff Forhan, good friend, avid reader, and fellow golfer, reads my manuscripts now and offers smart feedback, as does another friend, Arlo Kahn. My former agent, Cynthia Cannell, and my current agent, Marly Rusoff, have both been tremendously helpful, each in different ways. Marly has a particularly good editing eye, as do editors of recent books, Shaye Areheart, Chuck Adams, and Ina Stern. Two other fine writers, Sterling Watson and Dennis Lehane, stand as inspirations for me, and have been kind enough to invite me to teach at their Writers in Paradise conference at St. Petersburg's Eckerd College. With a recent novel, *A Little Love Story*, I asked my wife's reading group to read it in manuscript and make suggestions (This was done on impulse and was probably not the greatest idea I've ever had: it isn't easy to criticize a husband's work when the wife is sitting there, and, again, there were too many opinions involved). I won't mention by name all the good people who have been part of my writing life. If I tried to list all the friends who've been helpful to me in one way or another over the years I'd only end up forgetting someone. The list is long. The point is that, whatever success I have enjoyed, whatever credit I might deserve for surviving in the literary seas, needs to be widely shared.

The kind of good fortune I had in meeting friends like these and a mentor like Michael Miller is not as rare as it might seem. Most writers I know talk about a mentor, someone who came into their life at a key moment, helped them with a job, advice, or encouragement. In a money-minded world that can seem like an enemy to creativity, many people find small groups of like-minded writers, and within these groups life-long friendships often form.

It is important, I think, not to worry too much about finding a mentor or helpful friends. The rule here seems to be that if you persist in writing, if you approach it with the kind of sincerity and devotion with which you would approach a love relationship or a friendship you care about, then by some alchemy of the universe, a person, or several people, will likely come along to assist you. It is not wrong to reach out for this kind of help (though sending notes to writers you do not know and asking them to read your manuscript is probably not the best way to go about this. Most working writers have plenty to do in their own lives; some of them charge a fee for reading and editing, so having a stranger ask them to perform that task without pay — or, worse, sending a full manuscript to the writer's house, unsolicited — is something like a dentist being asked, by a complete stranger, to fill a tooth, gratis) but it might be wiser simply to devote yourself to the craft and then be alert for any help that happens to appear. As is true with other kinds of friendships, in some cases mentors serve a purpose only for a short period of time — until your first publication, say. In others, they continue to be indispensable for one's whole career.

It is important to keep in mind, however, that even the best advice, however generously offered, should be run through the filter of the writer's own sensibilities. This can involve difficult decisions. When you trust someone, the way I trusted Michael, it is often hard to know when to make use of their advice and when not to. While I'm convinced that no one writes a book entirely alone, it's also important to remember that what can make a book great is your uniqueness. Being too open to the advice of a mentor, teacher, or even an editor, can be as damaging to one's work as not being open enough. Trying to strike the perfect balance between what you believe to be good and what someone you trust believes to be good is one of the real challenges of the writing life.

Which brings us to the subject of criticism.

Demon Six
How Can They Say That About Me?

At every stage of a writer's career there will be criticism. How you deal with this inevitability is going to play a key role in your success or lack of success in the writing life. During the earliest stages of the writer's journey, as I mentioned in the chapter on choosing readers, this criticism will come from teachers or from those friends or relatives to whom you choose to show your work. In that sense, you have some control — over the source of the criticism, if not over the content. Later, if your work is published, the sources of criticism will sometimes be anonymous (as in on-line reader reviews and some pre-publication industry magazine reviews) and other times it will come from paid critics who do not know you personally. Though your ability to respond to these critics differs, the emotional impact they have upon your work may not.

More than once, when teaching in conferences and getting to know the people who had signed up for workshops there, I encountered writers who had experienced early criticism that was traumatic for them. To those who have never taken the risk of setting their private thoughts or the product of their imagination on the page, 'traumatic' might seem like hyperbole, but anyone who has ever ventured into the creative realm will understand. One of these writers told me she'd had such devastating criticism from a teacher in college that she'd abandoned her writing dreams for twenty years. It is an extreme case, but not particularly uncommon. Some writing teachers consider harshness a mark of honesty. They believe it is their duty — as if they are literary drill instructors, preparing soldiers for war — to toughen up their students by first breaking them down.

While this philosophy has been proven to work well in the Marine Corps — and even for some students — I have never liked it when it is applied to writers. Too often it serves as an excuse for the teacher to indulge his or her own sadistic or egotistical impulses, born of career frustrations, an excess of pride, bitterness, and jealousy. In some cases, yes, praise can be false, and excess or inauthentic praise can be harmful or at least a wasted opportunity. But writing is a difficult business, often solitary, always unpredictable, never measurable by any universally agreed-upon standard, and it has always seemed counterproductive to push the nascent writer's head under the water when he is out there drifting around in the shipwreck of failed sentences and false starts.

Here again, however, it comes down to individual taste. Some writers are not comfortable with kindness and want a strict master who points out mistakes without mercy. Those at the other end of the spectrum want only support and good words. Like choosing a genre that best suits your abilities, when you do have a choice of critics or teachers, it is helpful to work with people whose style matches your needs. Most writers will benefit from a constructive, supportive approach, at least in the first year.

In a workshop setting, this choice of what kind of criticism to solicit becomes more complex and more fraught with the opportunity for confusion. You are likely sitting in a room with as many as a dozen strangers and one published author. I never took a workshop myself, and took only two writing courses in college, but I have been the published author in this situation hundreds of times, and I have found it exceedingly rare to have anyone in the room who is bashful about offering an opinion. Writing is the only profession I know of in which those who are learning the profession are advised by others who are also learning it. I sometimes imagine a student in dental school practicing to pull a tooth, and having another student looking over her shoulder saying, "No, do it this way. Use a different grip. Pull harder!"

Of course there is a difference. We all know how to read and write, we've all been exposed to everything from great literature to popular best sellers, so it is more natural and more acceptable for non-professionals to offer each other advice. At the same time, I have heard some absolutely terrible suggestions tossed into the air of these classrooms, usually by people who have never come close to having their work published in a reputable journal, on a widely-read website, or by a good house. I remember one time — I was teaching at the Stonecoast conference in southern Maine — when a participant presented a wonderfully offbeat chapter from his novel and nearly every other writer in the room responded negatively. With as much diplomacy as I could muster, I tried to steer the comments into more favorable territory and, at the end of the class, bluntly stated my own opinion, but it was no sale. Everyone hated it. The author seemed perplexed. After the class, riding with him in an elevator up to the third floor of the hotel, I told him, "Listen, ignore every word you heard in there today."

Obviously, there is high quality criticism offered in some workshops, by students and teachers, both. At times, student writers in these situations are more apt to listen to their fellow students than they are to give credence to the teacher's remarks. I think that's a mistake. But what is valuable about the workshop environment is that it offers an opportunity to learn the necessary skill of filtering. The wisest writers in those situations listen respectfully to their fellows' comments (some teachers do not allow the writer whose work is being examined to speak at all in these sessions; I've never liked that idea) merely asking questions for clarification, to be sure they fully understand the criticism that is being offered. Then, in the privacy of their own creative environment, they ignore what they see as the bad advice, and embrace the good. Learning to discern the good from the bad is difficult, but it is an essential skill for the writer to cultivate.

This filtering skill remains important even after the

writer has been published; perhaps it becomes even more important then. Some agents offer criticism, some do not. In my experience, some are excellent editors and some are not. The agent's job is primarily to sell your work, to see that it is treated fairly in the monetary sense, and then to do whatever she can to ensure that it is widely publicized. My agent, Marly Rusoff, happens to be an excellent editor, as well as a fine saleswoman, and I always solicit and often heed her advice. I do know other writers, though, who, while they value their agent's skills at selling and promoting, ignore his or her literary suggestions.

I think it is a good policy, especially but not only in the first publication, to abide by what editors suggest. They almost always have a clearer view of the work than the creator does, and certainly have a better understanding of market exigencies. Most of them have an excellent ear for language, and a well honed understanding of what makes a book — or an article — work, or fail to work. If you have gotten an acceptance, or a tentative acceptance, for a magazine piece and you have little or no record of publication behind you, then you should do exactly what the editor asks you to do and not worry too much about tarnishing your artistic integrity. I have published hundreds of magazine and newspaper articles and it is still almost always the case that an editor will offer a suggestion that improves the piece or the novel.

If you are writing for class, there is no shame and little harm in making changes that correspond to what the teacher likes and asks for. But, outside of class, don't make the teacher into a god. If his criticism seems off-base or too harsh, do everything you can to ignore it — once you are free of the classroom dynamic. High school and college teachers, friends, agents, and magazine editors, can be absolutely wrong. Listen with an open mind, work hard to improve, but then, in your innermost self, in the quiet room from which your work originates, do what seems true to your vision.

In cases where you have a book contract and the manuscript has been accepted, it is especially important to keep to your vision of the work. This does not mean haughtily ignoring every suggestion that is offered, but it does mean carefully considering the advice and then setting it up against your idea of what the book is supposed to be. Even the most famous of editors can fail to understand what you are trying to do. Even brilliant editors can have a very different idea of what your novel is actually about, or of the way you want to structure your non-fiction book. These days, it is sometimes the case that editors do not have time for line-editing; once they've acquired your book, they feel — and their bosses feel — that their job is mostly done. If they do offer you detailed written criticism, it can be the result of one read-through.

The most difficult kind of criticism to deal with is the commentary of reviewers. Many people reading this book probably believe they would be overjoyed just to see their work reviewed. But I have found that the writer's dreams evolve, and tend to keep pace with the unfolding of actual events. At the start, all you'd like to do is finish the story or essay or novel you are working on. Then you'd like someone to read and enjoy it or be moved or enlightened by it. Then you'd like to see it published. Then you'd like to earn some money from it. Then, perhaps, you hope for widespread attention, praise, even fortune and fame. But at each of these stages you will have to balance your dreams against reality, decide whether to see the glass as half full or half empty. If you haven't published your book yet, you might think, "I don't care what they say, I just want to see it reviewed in the *New York Times*." But when that day comes, if the *Times* review is something less than positive, you might find yourself doing battle with the demon of bitterness.

I'm going to include two reviews here that I just received, literally four days before writing the first draft of this chapter. They are pre-publication reviews, one from *Booklist*, and the other from *Publishers' Weekly*. One, as you will see, is entirely positive, the other almost entirely negative.

Booklist:

The Italian Summer: Golf, Food, and Family at Lake Como.
Merullo, Roland (Author)

Apr 2009. 256 p. Touchstone, hardcover, $24.99.
(9781416563532). 914.5.

Imagine a Venn diagram connecting all those who love Italy, wine, food, family outings, and golf. The epicenter of those overlapping circles is not going to be all that large, but for anyone who lands there, this travel memoir delivers unadulterated joy. Merullo, the prolific author of an improbably wide range of fiction and nonfiction, wanted to slow the pace of his frenetic life by spending a summer with his wife and two daughters in Italy, not scurrying about from city to city but relaxing on Lake Como and indulging his passions for food, golf, and things Italian. His account of those idyllic weeks recalls Calvin Trillin in its casual tone, good humor, affable interactions with family, and everyman's love of regional food and wine.

But it's hard to imagine Trillin drawing a 260-yard drive around a dogleg or even four-putting from 20 feet for a double bogey. And, yet, even non-golfing gourmands will recognize that Merullo describes fairways and greens with the same kind of low-key charm and wit as he rhapsodizes over prosciutto and Pinot Grigio. A special travel book for a special audience.

Publishers Weekly:

The Italian Summer: Golf, Food, and Family at Lake Como Roland Merullo. Touchstone, $24.99 (256p) ISBN 978-1-4165-6353-2

In the summer of 2007, novelist and golf fanatic Merullo (Golfing with God; Revere Beach Elegy) set off with his family in search of the slower ways of life on the shores of Lake Como, Italy. Interspersing descriptions of various rounds of golf with trips to local restaurants and taverns, Merullo attempts to capture the sights, smells and sounds of the Italian and Swiss countryside. He recalls some of the characters that he and his family met that summer, such as Harold Lubberdink, real estate agent, who swept the family under his wing, leading them through various nooks and crannies of their temporary home country. Merullo takes readers on a harrowing journey through winding mountain roads in search of a perfect meal in a restaurant called La Baita. Finally, he tries to incorporate the slower pace of living into his own life, but finds it almost impossible. Part travel guide, part memoir, Merullo attempts to offer meditations on the richness of a life lived more slowly with good food and good company, but succeeds at little more than his frantic attempts to find a few good golf courses far away from home. (Apr.)

The critics can drive you crazy, if you let them. Not only is your ego involved, but in many cases their response to your work determines whether or not you will ever be published again, and what kind of advances you will receive for a future project if you are published. When my first novel, *Leaving Losapas*, was brought out by Houghton Mifflin in 1991, the editor and publicist did a wonderful job of garnering a lot of review attention for it. I remember very well that a prominent critic, Richard Eder, writing for the *Los Angeles Times*, said he thought the first section — set in Micronesia — was weak, and the second section — set outside of Boston in Revere, Massachusetts — was powerful. He cited examples and mounted a persuasive argument. And then, a week later, a reviewer in another paper — I believe it was the *Washington Post* — wrote exactly the opposite: how striking and original the first half of the book was, how predictable and flat the second.

No one escapes this kind of thing. *The Great Gatsby*, now universally recognized as a masterpiece, was published to decidedly mixed reviews in 1925, and sold only moderately well. Ask any published author — famous, mid-list, just building an audience — and they will tell you of good reviews and bad (usually being able to quote the bad ones verbatim.) In Hemingway's posthumously published novel, *The Garden of Eden*, the main character's wife mocks him for reading and re-reading reviews of his latest book. But few authors are able to ignore reviews entirely. I've gotten to the point where I read them once and then file them away. I do not want to hold too much harsh criticism in my mind, and I do not want to grow fat and indolent, licking the sweet frosting of praise. The bad reviews sting, of course. And the important bad ones more than sting.

When my third novel, *Revere Beach Boulevard*, was published, some of the reviews were wonderful. The book was one of five finalists for the prestigious L.L. Winship/PEN New England prize, went into paperback, and has been optioned for film by the actor Tony Musante. It was reviewed in the *New York Times Book Review*, and raved about in the *Washington Post Book World*, but my hometown paper, *The Boston Globe* — usually friendly to my work — ran a review that was sarcastic and without a single positive word. I remember sitting in a cafe in Stockbridge, Massachusetts, reading it and feeling crushed. This was a book I had put my heart and soul into, a complicated, multi-narrator suspense novel that centered around a young man with a terrible gambling addiction. It was set in my hometown, where I still had many relatives and friends. And, at that point, the Boston area was my fan base. While I have succeeded in blocking out the name of the person who wrote the review, I still remember its sarcastic tone and the sense that the reviewer had taken the work as a personal insult and lost all ability to be objective about its strengths and weaknesses.

Probably I did what I always did in those days (and still sometimes do) when I got a bad piece of writing news: when I got home I lay down in bed for an hour. During that hour, it was as if all the devils of mockery I'd ever encountered were rising up out of the carpet and circling the bed in a hideous dance, pointing fingers, laughing wickedly, citing my every failure and flaw. Gradually, the mood passed. I got up, grabbed something to eat, took a walk, had a conversation with my wife, watched a TV show, played a round of golf, did some house repair or mowed the lawn. The next day I was back at work; in time, the wound of the bad review slowly healed and left only a small scar. It would never be forgotten, but its power to keep me from writing would be reduced to zero.

If you cannot deal with this kind of intense disappointment, with public criticism — sometimes fair, sometimes not, sometimes completely confusing — then it's best to restrict your writing dreams to private journals. If you feel you are a highly sensitive person, take heart: you will likely grow a thicker skin as your writing career progresses. The kind of bad reviews that used to knock me down for a day, now only feel like a single punch. The bruise hurts for a while, but that's all. I am able to smile at the disparities like those in the examples above. As my former mentor, Michael Miller continually reminded me, "It's the work that matters. Just do the work. Just focus on that." It is a sentiment echoed by Truman Capote, who said, "Work is the only device I know of."

A last note on reviews: while it is important to be able to shake off bad criticism, especially when you truly believe it to be unfair or careless, in the early years a smart, careful reviewer can be of real value to you. Some of the criticism I recall from reviews of my first books still rings in my ears, but in certain cases the reviewer identified actual weaknesses in my writing, things I have since tried to repair or avoid. Don't be so disdainful of "the critics" that you entirely ignore the good ones. They sometimes work in tandem with the writer to produce a better end product.

Demon Seven
On Having Nothing to Say

I grew up in a vibrant neighborhood, surrounded by eccentric characters and a fair amount of violence. All during my childhood, I heard stories, sometimes very dramatic stories, in which real people suffered or triumphed. Later, I made it a point to have adventures, to travel, to work at a wide variety of jobs — taxi driving, parking cars, loading trucks, collecting tolls, building additions, coaching crew, teaching in college. Obviously, when I began writing books, this array of experiences gave me a wealth of material to draw upon.

The Demon we're describing here will tell you this is the only way to do it: have a lot of experiences, travel, suffer, take risks.

Not so.

Of late, it seems that the memoirs receiving the most attention are ones about childhood abuse, addiction, family disintegration and misery. While some of these — and novels based on similar events — are spectacularly good, and while I am grateful for having grown up in such a lively neighborhood, and for choosing to take risks and see the world when I was young, I think it is a mistake, a grievous mistake, to believe that one has to have a difficult or exciting life in order to write a good story.

I come across this often when I speak to students and one of them says, "I grew up in the suburbs and I had a nice, loving family. Nothing bad has ever happened to me, so I don't really have very much to write about."

These kinds of comments are sad to me on more than one level. The idea that any life lacks interesting events and characters strikes me as enormous failure of perspective. The idea that only memoirs of hardship and abuse have value is an idolatry of misery. Great books and essays have been written by people who never suffered any kind of childhood torment, never traveled the world, never worked at anything but the most mundane jobs. Wallace Stevens, great poet and insurance executive, comes to mind. And Emily Dickinson, a famous recluse. In an 800 page novel I love, *Oblomov*, by Ivan Goncharov, the main character barely leaves his bed for the entire book. In another of my favorite novels, *To The Lighthouse*, almost nothing happens that stands outside the boundaries of ordinary domestic life. And yet, the perspective that Virginia Woolf was able to take on those bland events, the psychological astuteness with which she was able to illuminate them, and the glorious prose in which she was able to describe them — all succeeded in raising the mundane to the level of the exquisite. She has a superb essay called "Street Haunting: A London Adventure", which describes a simple walk around a part of that city, ostensibly in order to buy a lead pencil. But she is able to see that common event from a perspective that recognizes the point of view of another great writer, Walt Whitman, who said, "To me every hour of the light and dark is a miracle." James Joyce's, *Ulysses*, widely recognized as one of the greatest novels ever written, describes a single day. While some of the characters are unusual, the events are decidedly ordinary, the kinds of things anyone might experience anywhere. Joyce was able to take that unpromising material and mold it into a work of genius.

We don't all have Virginia Woolf's abilities with prose, or Joyce's or Goncharov's brilliant imaginations, but the point is that a writer can never use an ordinary life, or a peaceful life, as an excuse for not being able to create. And it's not always suburban folk who believe their life to be too ordinary to write about. Richard Price, who grew up in the Bronx, and, at first, thought his life too common to write about, said, "with *Last Exit to Brooklyn*, I realized that my own life and world were valid grounds for literature, and that if I wrote about the things that I knew it was honorable — that old corny thing: I searched the world over for treasures, not realizing they were diamonds in my own backyard."

Everything is perspective. If you think your life has been boring, the people in it plain to the point of invisibility, then it will be impossible for you to make that life — or imagined scenes that grow out of that life — interesting to anyone else. It might even be impossible for you to see what is interesting in others' lives, real or fictional. This failure of perspective — exactly the opposite of Whitman's sense of the miraculous in everything — might be one of the most damaging demons of all. Unless a writer can find a way around it, success is highly unlikely.

One thing I like to do with students and workshop participants who complain of a lack of material is to ask them questions about their life, to have them describe the people and events in it. Sometimes it takes only a minute or two of this and a small bit of prompting to make them realize that, in fact, they have a great deal of material on which to draw. However, even if they persist in believing that their own experience was as boring as white toast with a butter substitute on it, if they can learn to observe carefully, to imagine fully, then they have a chance of creating something worth reading. For certain people, what matters is not eccentric personality or dramatic event, but intriguing ideas, and to that type of person, the wide world of writing opens its arms. They can craft an essay from a single idea, write a poem based on a thought, put together a book of musings that might sell a million copies.

(Strangely enough, as I was writing this section, my eight-year-old daughter came upstairs to talk to me about an idea for a story she is writing. As I did with her older sister, I teach a six-week writing course to her third-grade class. It's only an hour a week, and there are only a dozen kids or so who volunteer to take the course. At the end, we put together a book of their stories. These are boys and girls in public school, in a little country town in Massachusetts, people who have been alive only eight or nine years, yet they never seem to suffer from a lack of material.)

If you find yourself telling a teacher, a workshop facilitator, a friend, or a published author, that the reason you have never written anything is because you lack material, then consider recognizing this as just another demon. If you really do want to write, try setting your imagination free, opening the door of the cage of your supposedly boring existence and letting it swoop and soar in the world. Or try looking more carefully at the people and events around you, stripping away the disguise of familiarity, and finding the fascination that always lies behind it.

Demon Eight
I Cannot Do This Again

A week or so ago, I returned from a trip to Moscow. I had been invited by the American Embassy to come to Russia and speak to college students about writing and American literature. Before I stepped into some of those classrooms, teachers took me aside and asked a favor: would I mind emphasizing the idea that rewriting is necessary in order to create a good finished product? It amused me, because it is the same thing I hear, again and again, from teachers and professors on this side of the ocean before I talk to their students: please tell them how important it is to rewrite.

It's not important, it's essential. And not just in college.

I have a friend whose promising writing career was derailed by what might be called the Unable to Rewrite Demon. It is my understanding that Gertrude Stein suffered from this, too. Lover of literature that she was, writer of some natural talent, she was enamored of the art of composing and apparently incapable of doing the hard work of polishing.

I have a friend I will call Andrew, who wrote a novel

set in Paraguay, part adventure story, part love story. He asked me to read it. I went through the 400 pages with care, making marks and jotting down notes, and then we met in a restaurant for lunch and a talk. My feelings about the novel were almost entirely positive, but I knew there were a couple of bad habits to be addressed, and that certain sections and characters were significantly weaker than his best work. I suspected these flaws were the reasons why Andrew had not been able to get an editor interested in publishing the book.

We went through the novel chapter by chapter, knocking ideas back and forth. During the conversation, Andy seemed open to my thoughts. But then, at the end of the lunch, he said, "I just can't do this any more, Rol. I can't read it one more time. I've been working on the damn thing for three years now, I've rewritten it from start to finish six times, and re-read it probably fifty other times. I understand what you're saying but I just can't go back and rework it. I just can't."

The book was set aside and, despite his obvious talent, Andrew has never published it.

This reminds me of another friend, someone I'll call Mark. Mark's son, like Mark himself, was a fine athlete, especially gifted in soccer. In grade school and middle school his natural coordination and ability made him the star of the team, but in high school he turned out to be only an average player. It wasn't that his skills had deserted him or that he'd suddenly lost his coordination; it was that he'd cruised along on his gift and never developed it.

Less talented friends with a better work ethic, with more determination, had run, lifted weights, and spent extra hours at practice and they'd gone past Mark's son like geese flying past pigeons.

I've seen this so many times in writing students. I've had countless students with such a gift for language and storytelling that, while reading their work I felt spurts of envy. All but a tiny number of them have remained unpublished. There is certainly nothing wrong with remaining unpublished. It is neither a failure nor a disgrace. A career in journalism or book writing is not the only satisfying career, and for many people it is the wrong choice entirely. In fact, many writers I know advise beginners away from the profession: the odds of success are long; the odds of making a living at it even longer; the frustrations manifold. What's wrong, or at least sad, is to see someone like my friend Andy, who has the ability to write, and the desire to be a writer, but lacks the persistence and patience to tear his work apart again and again in order to make it as good as it can be.

For some writers, the thrill of composing is so great that they cannot make themselves do the rewriting, a stage that seems tedious in comparison. Understandable, but a crippling flaw. It is like hoping for a marriage that is all lovemaking and no dishwashing, all romantic dinners and no disagreements.

For others — and I am lucky to be one of these — while the composition stage of a novel is fraught with anxiety (Will I finish it? Will I get stuck? Let me get it out on the page before the computer crashes, the house burns down, I have a heart attack or die in a plane crash.) I love the process of painstakingly reworking a manuscript. I read through a book scores or even hundreds of times, always with pen in hand, making both small changes and large, incorporating or ignoring the advice of friends and readers, watching the work move closer to my vision of it. To me, a former carpenter, it is comparable to nailing cedar siding onto the walls of a new house, priming it, painting it, then painting the trim. It is painstaking, sometimes tedious work, but it is exactly what gives life and personality to the plywood-and-spruce structure that keeps out the rain.

There are various ways to overcome a natural disinclination to rewrite. One trick that works for some people is to take the medicine in very small doses. It can be daunting to think about going through a five hundred-page manuscript line by line, but the writer who works at book length has to learn to strategize in long chunks of time and work in small ones. Set yourself the goal of editing three or five or ten pages in a given session — perhaps composing another book in your other hours. Most people can edit ten pages in an hour or less, even allowing for some sticky spots and some daydreaming or walking around time. If you can put in five sessions during a week, you can have even a long manuscript edited in a few months.

Another suggestion is to recognize those days when the creative juices are not flowing, and use that time to go back over what you have already composed. Yes, in an earlier section, I advised those suffering from writer's block to push forward without stopping, but there is no rule that says you can't start the rewriting process until you have finished the entire manuscript. Sometimes when I'm writing a novel, I feel that I need to wait a short while to understand where the next section or chapter will take the story. Occasionally, I'll step away from the desk at these times, do something physical or read something inspirational. But sometimes I'll use this hiatus as an opportunity to go back and take another look at an earlier section, always with pen in hand, or, if I'm at the computer, always willing to make changes. This can be a way of killing two birds with one stone: you polish an earlier scene, and going over it helps you understand how to move forward.

It's important, in editing your own work, to realize that there is an inherent conflict of interest in the process: your mind is assessing the work of your mind. This can lead to a state of mental fuzziness, exactly the opposite of what you need to make a good revision. You can get to the point where you can't see whether a sentence is a good one or not, whether a character should say what he says, do what he does, or be in the book at all. This may be the point to ask one of your trusted readers to weigh in and give you a fresh look. If you are not ready for that, however, another trick is to set the pages aside for a day or a week or a month, or even several months, while you work on something else. After a couple of drafts, Truman Capote would put his work away for a week, a month, or sometimes longer. "When I take it out again," he said, "I read it as coldly as possible."

This may be difficult for students who have a great deal of homework and little time in which to finish an assignment. But it is another argument for starting things immediately rather than waiting until the night before they are due, or a day before the deadline.

Again, this may seem to contradict my earlier suggestion of plowing forward no matter what the obstacles. But there is no one right way of doing things. As T.S. Eliot said, in a comment I love: "I have found that different people have different ways of working and things come to them in different ways. You're never sure when you're uttering a statement that's generally valid for all poets or when it's something that only applies to yourself. I think nothing is worse than to try to form people in your own image."

It is a question of managing one's own interior situation, one's moods and tendencies. If you know you are prone to writer's block, then by all means push forward without stopping and save all the rewriting for a later time. But if you are confident that you'll get the piece finished, then you may be able to compose one day and edit the next, or compose for two weeks in a row, set the piece aside, take a break from writing, or work on something else, and then go back to the original material.

The danger in setting anything aside is that the thrill of the new pages will tempt you never to return to the old, so it is important to make a contract with yourself. Set a date when you will return to the manuscript and work on nothing but that.

During the editing process, which, lately, I have been saving until the first draft is complete, I'll sometimes print out a manuscript and carry it with me to a coffee shop, or some other fresh location. This is just another tool in the work box, another way of trying to gain a clear perspective on the material my own mind produced. I do not like to work in public, but on these occasions I'll find a quiet time and a quiet table and often it turns out that looking at the pages in a different environment gives me the kind of perspective on it that I could not get at home. Other times, I'll read through the manuscript much more quickly than my usual pace, or much more slowly. Or I'll open to the middle, pick a spot at random, and see how the page or the chapter seems. Or I'll read it aloud, sometimes imagining there is another person in the room. Any of these techniques can help provide a clearer perspective on your own work, and having that clearer perspective can help you develop a confidence in your ability to rewrite. That, in turn, will help you overcome the tendency to procrastinate, or to avoid editing altogether.

The ultimate goal of the rewriting process is to develop an internal editor, an objective-as-possible judge who enables you to see your own strengths and weaknesses. Of course, there will always be a blind spot. Just as we never really know what it feels like for others to be in our company, we will never really know what it feels like for another person to read our work. But, over time, over the course of years of listening to the advice and responses of trusted readers, agent, or editor, after thousands or hundreds of thousands of hours at the desk (or in the coffee shop) you can develop this internal editor to a degree that reduces the need for a lot of outside help.

Also, with time, we learn to avoid some of the pitfalls before they even get down on the page. This makes the editing process easier and more satisfying. To my surprise, teaching in college helped me with this. I had written for many years before I was offered a full-time teaching job. Once I started working at Bennington — work I limited to one semester per year so I'd have time for my own writing — I worried that talking about literature, and reading student work, would be detrimental to my own creative process. That turned out to be partly true. But, in addition to reading or rereading a number of great novels, and meeting some fine people, there was a benefit I did not anticipate: I got to see, first hand, how other writers reacted to criticism and suggestions. Again and again, when I found something in a student's work that needed to be changed or eliminated altogether, the student would respond as if he or she were in great pain. "Oh, but I love that section. I can't believe you want me to cut it!" Sometimes the love was completely misplaced: the section was awful, and the student could not see that. Other times, there really was something wonderful about the scene, but it broke up the flow of the story, or for other reasons just did not belong there. "You can never give yourself a break," Robert Stone said, "you always have to make the hardest decisions. That means, for example, writing a brilliant passage and then throwing it away if there is no use for it in terms of the total design."

"Kill your darlings," is a cliché of writing classes, and one I don't particularly like. It's akin, in my mind, to telling someone to break up with the person they seem to truly be in love with. In general, I'm suspicious of any kind of writing advice that supposedly applies to everyone in all situations. "Sometimes you have to kill your darlings," is the way I would prefer to put it. Seeing the reaction of students who had fallen in love with a character or a turn of phrase or a scene and were blinded by that love helped me to be aware of the tendency in myself, and, during the editing process, to be less reluctant to change or delete. In fact, as time has gone on, it has become much easier for me to cut out sentences or sections. I do it now without hesitation. If the deletion creates an ugly gap in the manuscript, I'm confident I can repair it. On a few occasions, thanks to a computer malfunction or an inadvertent keystroke, I have lost a few paragraphs or a few pages of work. At the time, this always seemed like a disaster, but in every case I can think of, when I rewrote the section from memory, it ended up being better than what had been lost. If you are really uncertain about removing a chapter you love, start a separate file for everything you cut out of the manuscript. When you've completed a draft, you can always go back to this file and see if any rubies or sapphires have been thrown into the trash.

Even the most highly refined internal editor cannot make rewriting obsolete. Jack Kerouac aside, there is no author I know of, or have heard of, who just spills things out on the page and never has to look at them again until they are in published form. We might have the fantasy of writing this way, but it is just that.

"Kill your unrealistic fantasies," is a piece of advice I can live with. Chief among those fantasies, a great temptation and a formidable demon, is the idea that the work, any work, is so superb the minute it is set down on the page that it never needs to be touched again. Think of a piece of your writing as a piece of music that must be rehearsed again and again before you have refined it enough to perform.

Demon Nine

Envy

Envy, one of the great demons, and one of the cardinal sins, can do more severe and lasting damage to the creative spirit than just about anything else I can think of. It is a powerful demon, one that returns again and again in various disguises, and one that has to be reckoned with from one end of the writing career to the other.

I have had many conversations with my good friend, Craig Nova, who has published eleven books, received a number of the most prestigious grants and awards in the American literary world, seen his work published internationally and praised widely, and made his living as a writer for four decades. In one of our talks, he mentioned a quote from the British statesman, John Fortescue, "Comparisons are odious." This has helped me in my life in general, and especially as a writer.

Envy always springs from dissatisfaction with oneself, or one's situation, and always arises from setting another self or situation against our own, and seeing our own in a dimmer light. It seems to be a natural aspect of living — or, at least, a natural temptation for most humans, but what has been surprising to me is to see how it works its evil magic at all levels of the writing life. It often seems true, as Aeschylus said, that "It is in the character of very few men to honor without envy a friend who has prospered."

In the early part of a writing career, a certain kind of reasonably healthy envy might arise from reading the work of a famous author, or hearing about his or her life (usually in a romanticized version where the disappointments, debts, failures, and struggles are seen in the light of eventual success), and wishing you had made that work, and lived — or were living — that life. A bit later, envy might show a slightly different face in a workshop or classroom, where the teacher makes a fuss over the work of your good friend or a complete stranger, and offers only a lukewarm enthusiasm for something you've put years into. On another level, it may happen that a person in your writing group secures a good agent, or announces that his book has been accepted for publication. Then, after you are published, it might be that you hear from another writer that he has an agent he adores, someone who has been able to sell his work to Hollywood and in a dozen foreign markets, or he has an editor who takes him to lunch at a fancy New York restaurant every few months. You might open the *New Yorker* one happy afternoon only to have your mood spoiled by a glowing review of a colleague's book (when the *New Yorker* has never acknowledged your existence). You know someone who has just won a grant you applied for unsuccessfully six years running, or who had a movie sale with a famous star and is spending the year in southern France working on a new book, while you have not yet earned out your modest advance and you're stuck in rainy Pocatello worrying about having enough cash to repair your drooping muffler. A former student of yours wins the National Book Award, and you are a mid-list author, publishing your sixth novel and still wallowing in literary anonymity.

It goes on and on. I remember so well being a novice writer, full of a passionate desire to be published, attending readings in order to learn everything I could about the business, to hear the kind of language I wanted to use, to see what I did not want to write, and how I did or did not want to act in public forums if I ever got the opportunity. In the question and answer periods that followed these readings, the writer would sometimes be heard to complain about how exhausting his book tour was, the look-alike hotels, the plane flights, the time away from family. And I would think, I'd give anything to be able to have a book tour, to be published, to be able to use the words "my agent" or "my editor", to go to New York for a meeting with someone who wanted to talk about my novel. I'd give anything to walk into a bookstore and see my creation up there on the shelf, to receive a fan letter, or a royalty check — no matter how small.

But then, when the time came that I did get a book published, and had a book tour, and then another book and another tour, and then another, I caught myself starting to complain about the low publicity budget, the look-alike hotels, the time away from family. I tried not to let the words escape in public because I did not want to sound like the writers I'd listened to so many years before, but I felt the same thing they had been feeling. My achievement level had been matched and sometimes exceeded by my dissatisfaction level.

Envy is about dissatisfaction, and the opportunities for dissatisfaction are ubiquitous and never-ending. For some writers, no amount of success is enough. I am personally acquainted with wealthy best-selling authors who are miserable because they have never won certain awards, or been admitted to certain prestigious literary societies. For others, the inherently unjust nature of reviews and publishing success becomes absolutely intolerable, and their creative spirit burns up in a fire of bitterness.

Forget about the glass being half-full or half-empty: from the start of your writing career you should work to cultivate an appreciation for there being anything in the glass at all. This is exceedingly difficult; for some people entirely impossible. But it is, I believe, an attitude to strive towards and one that will only energize your writing spirit. You can look at all those who are more successful than you. . . and be miserable. Or you can look at all those who would love to have what you have...and be thankful. Or, hardest and best of all, you can learn not to pay so much attention to what others have and don't have, learn to stop placing yourself on a spectrum, and just be grateful that you are physically and mentally able to write a story or a book of poems or an essay; and then that you've had something published; and then that you've made some money from it and given pleasure to a few hundred, a few thousand, or a few million readers.

I hear the whispers of the demon of envy on a regular basis. I'll read a review of a writer I know, someone whose work I'm familiar with, and the review will be filled with such glowing praise that I'll feel the demon swell up between my ears. Your work is at least as good, it will say, really much better, so why didn't you get lavish praise like that for your most recent novel? She made hundreds of thousands from that sappy romance; here you are, writing serious literature and scraping by. The thoughts go on and on.

Most days now I am able to follow my mentor's sound advice, just let the work be the focus, and forget about the awards and accolades. This is complicated by the fact that I earn my living writing, and support my family that way, so a bad review is more than just a blow to the ego; it can have a very real bearing on our family finances.

But I try to wrestle the demon of envy to the dirt. I look at everything I have: work I love, a good publication record, a house with a wonderful wife and kids, some travel. Yes, I have made sacrifices and worked hard, and yes there have been a long list of failures, physical troubles, bad breaks and unfair results over the past thirty years, and thousands of hours of financial uncertainty, loans, bills, and worry; and yes, many people have more than I do. But there have also been acts of great generosity from other writers to me, the kindness of critics, the effort of agents, editors, publicists and booksellers, and many strokes of pure good fortune.

It is essential to remember that there is always an element of fate involved in bookselling, and that this element often has little or nothing to do with the quality of your work. One of my novels, *Breakfast with Buddha*, has had foreign sales, a nice film option, gone into multiple printings, and sold over 100,000 copies — eight times more than books I put as much or more effort into, books that had better reviews, a larger publicity budget, books in which I had invested more hope. Even the most experienced editors and marketing directors do not really know what makes a book commercially successful. Some of it is talent, some of it is hard work, some of it is timing, some of it is a wise choice of genre or subject matter, some of it is the effort and resources of publisher, editor, and agent. But a lot of it is just luck, or fate, or karma, and it is one of the writer's great challenges to do whatever he or she can do to make a book — or a career — successful, and then have the good grace to accept what happens. Or at least try to do that.

This is a moral issue, but it is also a practical one. While a degree of envy can often be used to motivate us in a healthy way (I want to write a book as good as *The Great Gatsby*, or *To The Lighthouse*; I want a house in southern France; I want to be invited to join the Academy of Arts and Letters), it is more likely that envy will end up pouring fuel on the fire of bitterness, and I do not know of many writers who produce good work from the land of bitterness. I do not know of anything that is helpful and useful in the habit of constant comparison.

Writing, to me, is not a competitive sport. I rarely read the *New York Times Book Review* (anymore), or any reviews at all. I make it a point never to look at others' books on Amazon.com to see how they are selling, and what kinds of reviews they are getting. I try to be supportive of my writing friends, going to their appearances when I can, buying their books to read and to give as gifts, saying good things about them and their work. Though I confess to feeling the tug of envy as much as anyone, I strive to be sincerely glad for their success, and I have an odd little practice: whenever I hear of someone who had great writing news, I say, "I'm happy for them. I wish them well." In some cases I mean that. In other cases not so much. But it is a way, without denying the real stirrings of envy, to work against them rather than indulge them, and I find that this always redounds to my own benefit, giving me a more hopeful and positive attitude toward my own work, toward the life of writing and reading, and to this complicated, sometimes unfair and frustrating business.

Demon Ten
Wishful Thinking

This is a strange demon, recognizable when the intense longing to "be a writer" is not matched by a willingness to make any sacrifices toward that end. Sacrifice is something that comes more naturally later in a career, when there have been publications, when writing has become a source — possibly the source — of income. But even early on, when you are still building a career, perhaps still unsure that there will be any publications at all, it is essential to sacrifice something. Think of a love relationship. Once you are dating someone regularly, engaged or married to them, or have children with them, it is natural to make sacrifices for them. These selfless acts are so much a part of any good relationship that we often cease to see them as sacrifices. We'll pick up our lover's clothes at the dry cleaner, bring him or her a milkshake during a hospital stay, help him figure out a checkbook or computer problem, listen to her complain about work, massage a sore back or ankle.

In the early going, though, it's not so natural. At some point we have to give up dating others, or give up our regular Saturday night game of pocket billiards, or give up thinking only about ourselves, and make a commitment to the other person, to the relationship. Along with the pleasures it brings, this commitment involves some sacrifice.

It is exactly the same with writing. Once you decide it is something you want to take seriously, your writing will exact a payment in time and effort. There will be times when you have to skip a party you want to attend, or give up the luxury of sleeping late on a Saturday morning, in order to find time to write. I often tell students that they have to create a "sacred space" for their writing. It is usually not enough to just write when you feel like it or when it is convenient. Some discipline is called for, and part of that discipline involves keeping a part of your day or your week just for writing and letting nothing short of an emergency interfere.

I know a mother of three with a full-time job who gets up at five in the morning in order to have a couple of hours of writing time. I know people who have had to tell their spouses, boyfriend or girlfriend, that they are going to carve out four hours on a Saturday in order to write, and so won't be able to go kayaking or contra-dancing the way they used to. I have a younger friend who quit his secure high school teaching job, left his apartment, moved into his in-laws' basement, endured a long period of alienation from his parents, and devoted himself to a novel for several years. After a number of rejections and dead ends, his novel was published by a highly respected house, the book was optioned by a famous movie company; my friend and his wife moved into their own apartment, he is well on his way to a successful career (and his wife has since published a novel, as well!).

Would that have happened if he'd kept his secure job, tried to please his parents, and written only an hour or two here and there?

These kinds of sacrifices are always difficult, especially when they bear on a person's finances. When I was offered a full-time, year-round teaching position at Bennington College ("a dream job" one fellow writer told me) I declined and decided to work only half the year. From a financial standpoint, this was truly foolish, but it was a way of nurturing my writing life. I'd published two books at that point, but I had the sense that if I worked full-time reading others' writing, commuting to the college, preparing classes, I'd lose my momentum. Fortunately, I had an understanding wife who was willing to take the risk of enduring money worries in order to let me try to do what I dreamed of doing: making a living from writing alone. When the time came for me to leave Bennington (for reasons that had nothing to do with my sacred writing time) we had a two-year-old and Amanda knew we were letting go of our one regular source of income. But there was no hesitation in her. Every year since leaving the academic world, I've made more money than I would have had I stayed.

Sacrifice is an easy word to say, a simple concept. Somehow, though, when we actually face it in real life, there is pain involved, and that pain is not abstract. Some people have such an abundance of time and money that the kinds of sacrifices they need to make seem small to the rest of us, but, really, this is not true. Even for such fortunate souls, writing does not come magically. Success almost always arrives after years of work. We see the successful writer on stage or on television, being interviewed, receiving an award, signing books, and it is easy not to see what lies behind that moment, a long string of giving things up to secure that sacred time.

The demon, in this case, entices us to wear the disguise of ambition and passion, without the flesh and blood that is the work.

Demon Eleven
Lack of Time

Which brings us to the issue of time management, another aspect of the writing life that is not so much about technical skill as it is about mental organization and discipline. Again, there are, no doubt, some people reading this who do not have to worry about a lack of time or financial resources, but for most writers — students and professionals, alike — finding time to indulge their passion means working it in around domestic or career responsibilities, financial obligations, or the demands of coursework. This juggling act is rarely a simple matter. One of the real benefits of college writing programs, M.F.A.s and the like, is that they provide a year or two of writing time. True, there are ancillary requirements at most programs, and some students have to work to help pay the way, but at least writing can take center stage for those years. For most people, that is a luxury.

Even more luxurious is time at a writer's colony. In the first years of my career, I had the very good fortune of spending a wonderful month each at the Edna St. Vincent Millay Colony and the Blue Mountain Colony, both in upstate New York. Thirty days in beautiful surroundings, meals provided, and quiet space set aside, all in the service of time to create. I've never gotten so much work done in such a short period. Even there, though, some of the fellows could not manage their time and frittered it away in gossip and false starts, in what they thought of as "networking", treating the residency as pure vacation, fooling themselves into thinking they were furthering their careers that way. I don't mean to sound too harsh here — I had good times at those places, too, and several of the other residents worked as hard or harder — but for someone who had been squeezing out a few writing hours here and there for years, it was a surprise to see how creatively creative people could misuse a valuable opportunity.

Students are immersed in the busy whirl of school, with academic and social considerations, so writing time comes at a premium for them, as it did for me when I had a full-time carpentry career. Many of the writers I encounter at conferences are raising children, managing a home, or holding down the other kind of full-time job. In such cases, too, time for writing is scarce, energy can be in short supply, and there is an almost unlimited list of potential excuses to pull you away from the desk: everything from a clogged sink to a friend's phone call to a favorite TV show. It is important, in such a complicated life, to have a system that guarantees you some writing time. This can be as simple as setting aside certain hours — Monday, Wednesday, and Thursday nights from 8 to 11; Saturday afternoon from 1 to 6 — or as complicated as squeezing in a burst of work when your sixteen-month-old is napping, taking advantage of every free half-hour the week presents.

In the years leading up to the acceptance of my first novel, I was building a one-man carpentry business in western Massachusetts and clinging, sometimes desperately, to the dream of the writing life. I felt caught in a vise: if I didn't have much carpentry work, there was an abundance of time to write but not enough money to pay the bills; if I did have a lot of carpentry work, the writing time and energy were squeezed down almost to zero. I remember having conversations with Amanda about it, venting my frustration, my impatience, my urgent desire to be published. Where this desire comes from is a mystery; its source varies from person to person, but the urgency is something I recognize immediately in the voices and faces of workshop participants, students, and friends.

It may be true that the people who feel this urgency, if they manage it well, have the best chance of ultimately succeeding in the writing world. Managing it well can be compared to adjusting the flame on a gas stove or an outdoor grill — too low and the flame goes out entirely; too high and it becomes destructive, licking over the top of the frying pan and scorching whatever lies inside. To keep it at the proper intensity, I think it is important to write regularly. But it is most assuredly not important to write every day. In fact, telling a beginning writer that he or she must write every day is the kind of too-certain advice that can mutate into another demon. The writer can't manage that, and feels guilty, and wonders if she has sufficient motivation. This spiraling negative thought pattern saps the writing energy.

Everyone with a true passion develops his or her own schedule. T.S. Eliot found that he could be productive for only about three hours at a stretch, usually in the middle of the day. Susan Cheever works best when she wakes up from a night of sleep or a nap. Norman Mailer wrote for six hours in the middle of the day, three days a week. Certainly, in the intervening hours he was musing about his work, perhaps making an outline, pondering, letting his subconscious grind away on the material. But his actual at-the-desk time was nothing like the daily pattern some advisors insist on. Phillip Roth writes every day from 9 to 5 as if he has an office job. Obviously, that works for him. The point here is to find out what works for you, and not to be hamstrung by someone else's idea of a healthy writing schedule. Going too long between sessions is a good way to let the fire die out, but for many people, long stretches of work or a set-in-stone daily schedule is impossible.

When my carpentry business grew to the point where I had regular work — sometimes larger projects that involved six-day weeks for six or eight months at a time — I always tried to write a little bit every day so I did not lose contact with the people in my novel. At lunch hour, I'd make notes on pieces of 2 x 6, or sit in the cab of my van or pickup, scribbling a paragraph into a notebook. Once work was over for the day, I'd drive home, have dinner with Amanda, wash the dishes, then go down into that half-finished corner of our basement and write for half an hour or an hour or an hour and a half — until I was too tired to be working effectively. On weekends and rainy days, I'd try to put in four or five hours, often more. I was lucky to have such an understanding spouse, and lucky to be able to channel the urgency in some kind of a regular fashion.

Once I published a couple of books and landed a teaching job, I found it more, not less difficult to write. The academic life, with its undercurrent of dissension and oversupply of meetings, with all the pages of student writing to read, and all the classes to prepare, was not, for me, a good complement to the writing life. I found I could get almost no serious writing done during a semester of teaching, and this made me feel frustrated and impatient, which created a nice atmosphere for the demons. (For more cerebral types, all that reading is stimulating; I preferred to bang nails.)

Our children are still young — 12 and 8 as I write this — and both Amanda and I try to spend as much time with them as we can. This might mean meeting them at the end of the school day and going out for ice cream, or taking a hike in the snowy woods. In warmer weather, it can mean a trip to the lake for an afternoon swim, or a game of soccer or golf. We have the usual driving commitments of modern American parents — to ballet, girl scouts, music lessons. In this stage of life I have had to let any thought of a regular schedule fly up into the air like a released birthday balloon. Now I write whenever I can, going to my desk for an hour before bed, or on a Saturday morning, or most of a full day when the girls are at school. I have learned not to fret about this — somehow, the work always seems to get done. And, over the years, I have gotten much more efficient. The internal editor I spoke of in another chapter has matured to the point where less and less of what I put on the page in a first draft needs to be excised later on. The work is not perfect, obviously, and there are still false starts and failed projects, but it is better than in the early years, I hope, and I am sure that it comes forth more easily. There is a lot to be said, in any profession, for the lessons learned from 30 years of making mistakes.

One trick I often use, say on a night when I am tired, the girls went to bed late, and I have to force myself to go upstairs to my desk, is to say to myself, "Just write half a page. Anybody can write half a page." I'll sit down with that goal in mind and almost always produce a page or two. Whereas if I told myself, in that tired state, that I had to get two pages done before going to bed, I probably wouldn't go to the desk at all.

Unless you are working two jobs and doing all the cooking and cleaning and have three children at home to care for, or unless you or someone close to you has a chronic illness that requires constant care, I think there is probably a portion of your life that you can regularly devote to writing. If you have an infant who doesn't sleep, and a spouse who doesn't help, or if you have a depressed relative who needs a lot of commiseration, then of course there isn't going to be much writing time or energy available. In most cases, as time passes these kinds of situations change. The thing to watch out for is telling yourself you have no time when, in fact, you do. And telling yourself you are really committed to writing if you aren't proving that by sitting at the desk for some hours every week.

If you know you won't have a lot of time, make a wise choice as to what kinds of things you want to write. This might mean switching to a shorter genre, or avoiding projects that require voluminous research. If you happen to have the luxury of a stretch of time with only a few obligations scheduled, then it makes sense to begin a novel or a complex work of non-fiction. Keep the long view. Remember, if you manage to write only six pages a week but maintain that output, you'll have 300 pages at the end of a year.

What I'm saying here is that many different obstacles can appear between a writer and a finished piece of work. Don't add to them by poor thinking, poor time management, by making decisions that set you up for failure, or by putting illogical pressure on yourself to accomplish a heroic amount under difficult circumstances. Manage your interior world in such a way that it makes it easier to manage your time.

Part of this involves learning the tricks that bring you more easily into a writing frame of mind, especially if your writing time comes in shorter segments. Annie Lamotte talks about what she calls her pre-writing "aerobics". She sits down to write and realizes she needs to wash the dishes. She sits down to write after the dishes are washed and realizes she has to feed the cat. Sits down after the cat is fed and realizes she needs to send an email, etc. Richard Price spends the first hour at his desk reading the newspaper and answering phone calls. In both those cases, as in mine, these small errands serve not as distractions but as warm ups. I know when I sit down to work and start out by looking at emails and answering a couple of them, that this is just foreplay. I can feel the writing energy building. I don't make the mistake of continuing with the e-mails for half an hour or an hour or two hours when I know I should be working on a book.

Some people go out and take a long walk as a way of getting ready, or they do a brief meditation. In his inspiring book, *On Becoming a Novelist*, John Gardner says that whenever he reached a place where he was stuck, he would go to his workshop and make a set of shelves. It doesn't matter how you get into, or back into, the writing state of mind. What matters is that you don't turn these exercises, in the end, into distractions, but use them as preparation, or as a bridge between productive periods. When you reach the end of them — and that should usually be a matter of minutes, not hours, you should be like a pitcher who has been warming up and is now ready to start the game. No more fooling around. Begin.

In this, as in so many other of the demon-fighting techniques, it is essential to cultivate and maintain a positive frame of mind. Writing is difficult, yes. But you have to decide in advance that the difficulty is worth it; you want to write that badly. Once you've made that decision, try not to second guess. Go forward with confidence, sure that you can repair whatever mistakes you make along the way, sure that you are gradually getting better, sure of your self-discipline, all the while understanding that the management of your interior world is a difficult skill that takes years of honing.

Demon Twelve
Self-Limiting

Setting goals is a good way to counteract the demons. From the start, my strategy has always been to set my goals very high, to try with all my energy and will to reach them, and then to be satisfied wherever I end up. I remember telling my first editor, at Houghton Mifflin, that my dream was to make a living only from writing. "Oh, hardly anyone is able to do that, you know," she said. I knew that, of course, but when I heard those words a part of me responded, silently, "But that's my dream, and unlikely as it may be, I am going to try for it." In ten years time, that dream came true.

And I remember, when I first started to take golf seriously in my mid-forties, telling a golfing friend that I wanted to one day be a single-digit handicap. "The chances of that get smaller every year, as you get older," he said, as if I'd told him I wanted to win an Olympic wrestling medal. Right, true, absolutely true. But I tried and tried and eventually attained that humble goal. Nothing particularly special about it, there are millions of better golfers. But the point is I wasn't about to limit myself before I even really tried.

These days, I tell myself I would like to win the Nobel Prize in Literature. I know precisely how unlikely that is, but that isn't the point. This isn't an exercise in dealing with reality, this is an exercise in self-motivation. Writing something, I will sometimes tell myself, "this is going to win the Pulitzer." I do this, not out of conceit, but as a way to counter the tendency I have toward an excess of doubt — something that could cripple my writing spirit. I know people who limit themselves before they even begin. They're sure they will never be published. Well, it's true, the odds are long, but people do get published. Why are those people inherently more likely to get published than you are? If you want to get published, then believe in the possibility, try as hard as you can, hold fast to the dream, and if it happens, celebrate with all your might (Craig Nova gave me this good advice years ago: make sure to mark every piece of big good news. Buy a shirt or a leather jacket, go out for a special meal, anything to remember the occasion by. In my family, we have the odd tradition of running around the outside of our house with no clothes on when good news arrives from New York. Fortunately, we are surrounded by thick woods.)

If that good news never arrives, then at least you tried, which is more than a lot of people can say.

If you try and try and keep failing, year after year, then only you can decide if it's time to alter the dream, give it up entirely, or keep working. There are dozens upon dozens of writers who failed for years before succeeding. Read the biography of the British writer Barbara Pym, for one good example, or the story of the publication of William Kennedy's novel, *Ironweed*. Rejection upon rejection, in both cases, and then, after years of persistence, great success.

Between 1978 and 1991 I had almost nothing in the way of success, a couple of magazine and newspaper acceptances, scores of rejections, maybe $3,000 earned in thirteen years. I was a finalist for half a dozen grants without winning any of them (I still have not had much success with grants.) To me, it was worth it to keep going. I had enough encouragement from my wife and my mentor, just enough self-belief. I made just enough money from other work, and that gave me just enough time to keep writing. Friends helped in a variety of ways, but I kept going. If you decide not to keep going, there is absolutely nothing wrong with that! Find another dream and transfer your passion to it. But I like to remember the quote from Goethe that I used as an epigraph for my first novel. "It occurs to me that the hope of persisting, even after fate would seem to have brought one back to a state of nonexistence, is the noblest of our sentiments."

Demon Thirteen
Impatience and Rejection

No one likes to be rejected, and not many people like to wait, but, in all its various stages, the writing life will probably require you to deal with the former and endure the latter. Two of my writer friends experienced what might be called "instant success" — though, of course, it came after years of work. A few days or a few weeks after sending off their novels they landed a good agent, and very soon after that the agent was able to sell their books. In both cases these writers had to endure rejection, but that came after this initial, quick success. Probably, in the history of letters, there are a handful of authors whose careers had no dark spots in them, no form letters saying "Sorry, not right for us", no bad news over the telephone or in the mail. A very small handful. The vast majority of us have had our dreams knocked to the pavement and trampled on, again and again. I will say about rejection the same thing I said about criticism: if you cannot find a way to deal with it, you should choose another line of work, another dream.

As is true with the other demons, there are various tricks for dealing with rejection. (I like to remember a good friend's story that has nothing to do with writing. She told me once that, when a beloved boyfriend broke up with her, she went out and bought herself a lobster dinner she could not really afford. It was a kind of revenge.) A poet friend keeps a stack of addressed manila envelopes on his desk. When a poem gets rejected, he puts a fresh copy in one of these envelopes and immediately mails it off to another magazine — which gives him no time to dwell on the failure.

Some people get furious and storm around the empty house cursing the foolish editor who failed to see the high quality of their work. Some people cry. Some people quit . . . for a day or a week or a month, or forever. I find that my own reaction is often delayed: at first, I tell myself it doesn't matter and I just keep on working. Days or weeks later, though, the rejection and its consequences sink in and then I have to do battle with several of the demons at once. For me, rejection has become somewhat easier to absorb since I've compiled a record of publication, some good sales, some good reviews. Kind letters from readers are like good meals, strengthening the body against the day when influenza strikes in the form of a No from a publisher or editor. Still, a record of good reviews is no bulletproof armor — as I found out recently when a novel I'd been partly paid for was rejected by a publisher I'd worked with for years. It hurt, financially and emotionally . . . though not quite as much as it would have years ago.

My first big rejection, and still the most memorable one, came when I was trying to get my first novel published. I had been working on it for four or five years, and, thanks to my friend Dean Crawford, had found an agent to represent it. (Even that good fortune came only after a number of other agents had said no.) She had gotten several rejections on the manuscript, but then called me one summer Friday and said that an editor at Houghton Mifflin had read the first half of the book and loved it. "He's going to read the second half over the weekend," she said. "I'll call you the minute I hear from him."

Saturday and Sunday passed very slowly. I had been writing seriously for more than ten years at that point, and when I lived in Boston I had often walked past the Houghton Mifflin building on Park Street, seen photographs of their authors in a glass case near the door, and, in better moments, imagined myself there. On Monday, when the agent called, she had bad news: the editor had not liked the second half of my novel, and was not going to make an offer on the book. "I know how disappointed you are," she said, "but he wants to speak with you. It's very rare for an editor to offer to do that, so I hope you'll give him a call."

Disappointed wasn't the word. I was crushed. But after sulking for a while, I did call the editor and I spent half an hour listening to him tell me what he thought was wrong with the second half of the novel. The main problem, he said, was that I had inserted a new person between the reader and the main character. I had done that, the editor believed, because I was trying to keep the difficult events of the second part of the book at arm's length. I was afraid of those feelings, he thought, but it was, in fact, the power of those same feelings that had the potential to move readers, if I could bring myself to face them head on. "These are just my thoughts", the editor said. "Someone else might see it differently."

Before the conversation was half finished, I knew he was right. I hung up the phone, felt sorry for myself for another day or two, and then began the process of entirely rewriting the second half of the novel. It took several months, and was probably the most difficult work I have ever done, but when it was finished, I hand-delivered the novel to the Houghton Mifflin building (the secretary there would not let me get anywhere near the editorial offices), and a few months later they bought it.

Most of the agents I've dealt with or heard about over the years have a tremendously difficult time passing on bad news to their authors. I know one agent who waits until she has some good news to balance the bad, and only then will she call or email her author and let the hammer fall.

What helps most, I find, is simply realizing that you are not alone. Certainly you will feel alone. Most likely the rejection — whether it is from the local newspaper or the National Endowment for the Arts, for a first novel or a tenth — will encourage the negative voices and refresh the pain of old wounds. Let it be. Let the demons wail and the pain surge; let it paralyze your writing muscle for a while and don't worry too much about it. Mourn, scream, drink, sulk, play video games — whatever gets you through.

But at some point not too long after the arrival of the bitter news, you need to fight back against those feelings. Go back to the desk, even if only for an hour at first. Curse the editors as you work, imagine great things for yourself, speak to the framed photograph of Rocky Marciano on your wall, but don't walk away. If you read the biographies of famous writers you will see that few if any of them were protected from the poisonous feelings engendered by rejection. You are not alone. The work itself, with its challenges and satisfactions, its therapeutic release of subconscious material, is a well that nothing can poison.

In good days and bad, there have been many times when I've walked around my house singing the Tom Petty lyric, "The waiting is the hardest part." Not as hard as rejection, I think, but it is often true in the writing profession that things happen slowly, and this can make the writer feel he is hungry and walking through waist-deep hardening cement toward the counter where the food is being served.

It ended up taking twelve years from the time I committed myself to writing until the time that first novel, *Leaving Losapas*, was published. You will not hear me saying that was an easy time, that I knew all along it would work out well in the end, or that there weren't periods of discouragement and despair.

But even after that first publication, there have been stretches of empty time while I waited to hear from my agent about a book she was submitting, or waited to hear from a magazine editor, or waited to get paid for something that had been published months earlier, or waited to learn whether or not I had won a grant, a residency, a prize. The demons love these empty times. Try as you might to seal the cracks, you have to allow a little space for the news to arrive, and the demons somehow know how to slip in through that space and surround you.

It is also difficult to know how long to wait, say, for an answer from a new agent to whom you have sent your materials. My feeling is that the busiest person on earth ought to be able to give you some kind of a response within a month or six weeks; if you haven't heard by then, it is perfectly appropriate to make a polite inquiry. If that inquiry doesn't yield results, there is no reason not to send the materials elsewhere. Agents who demand exclusive reading rights ought to read and respond promptly, but the business is littered with editors and agents who fail to treat writers with basic respect, and it is important to fight back against this kind of treatment.

There are times, though, when you can do nothing to speed up the process, and you just have to simmer in a stew of anticipation, pushing back the negative possibilities with your positive imaginings and trying to keep the flame of hope burning. Without question, the best thing to do in this situation is to work. While you are waiting to hear from that agent, start another book, or a shorter project. Like John Gardner, you might have several novels ready by the time the first is accepted. If nothing else, you will have kept the more serious, crippling demons at bay, and made good use of the waiting time. As is true with criticism and rejection, periods of waiting are just part and parcel of the writing profession. No one likes it. Often the agent or editor at the other end of the silent phone line really is overwhelmed with work — or perhaps he or she has personal problems or health issues. It is not easy to cultivate the virtue of patience, least of all when the flame of your passion for writing is burning hot, or when you feel you might be on the cusp of a big career break-through. Nor is it a simple matter to strike the correct balance between being appropriately patient, and not let-ting yourself be taken advantage of. As with other interi-or management skills, every writer figures out this puzzle in his or her own way. I mention these demons here only so that you might be prepared for them, and realize that many others are dealing with them, too.

Demon Fourteen
Success

Now we come to the demon of success, a strange and sly fellow who arrives at your doorstep dressed in fine clothes, spouting kind words, but one who can still rob you of your writing energy. To those who have not yet been published, it might seem odd to have to start worrying about the temptations that accompany success, but it is not a bad thing to have a small warning sign ready in the back of your mind when the big day comes.

First, as I touched upon earlier, success is defined differently for different people. For some, just being able to finish a project, no matter how modest, is a mark of forward movement. I remember finishing a play, somewhere about 1981, and feeling a powerful sense of satisfaction. The play never left the house; I don't believe I showed it even to Amanda. I had never written a play before and have never written one since, and I don't even remember what this one was about. But I finished it. Over a period of a couple of months, I had held the voices of doubt at bay long enough to keep working on that project, to get to the end of it. Step one.

For others, success might simply mean writing a few

pages that give a little pleasure to someone else. Maybe it is a ten-page account of a recent trip to Korea, or a memoir about childhood that can be shared with siblings. Maybe it is a collection of humorous poems, or an adventure tale, or a story written for one's five-year-old daughter. That might be enough for you, enough to justify the hours invested and the sacrifices made . . . and the cost of that writers' conference in Santa Barbara next summer.

Others have greater ambition — to be published, to be widely read, to become famous, to make a fortune. As long as it does not sap you of your motivation, it is probably wise to remember that the odds of becoming famous and making a fortune from writing — or anything else — are extremely long. Even the odds of getting a book published by a well known house are daunting (increasingly, some people are happy to self-publish; more power to them. Some of them have sold millions of copies of their work). Pretending otherwise would be like pretending that finishing a marathon is the same as jogging around the block. That kind of attitude will not help you in the fourteenth mile.

It is true, however, that success does come for many thousands of writers, and that, if you don't train for and enter the marathon, the chances of finishing are not remote, they are nonexistent. While you might never be famous in the sense that movie celebrities and athletes are famous, you might indeed have a book — or many books — published, might be asked for your autograph (at least on the title page of your novel), appear on local or national

TV, or be interviewed for a magazine. If you want proof of the possibility of success, just walk into the nearest bookstore.

But if success does come to you, after a year or many years of effort, what effect will it have on your work, and on the interior world from which that work springs? Some successful authors become so enamored of the trappings of literary acknowledgment that it turns into an end in itself. They start seeing themselves from the out-side. They start thinking of themselves as the person who is written about in the newspaper. I've been at parties with successful authors where, instead of looking at the person they are talking to, their eyes flit over the crowd, watching for another famous soul to mirror them, or they look anx-iously here and there, expecting adulation. They begin to believe they are somehow above the ordinary human du-ties and frailties. Yes, it's true, I throw my laundry all over the place and expect my wife to pick it up, and yes, she complains about it, but did you see what they wrote about my latest book in the *London Times*? Yes, my son or daughter would like to spend time with me, but there are fans out there waiting for my next work, isn't that more important?

After a successful book, advances can go way up, but so can the expectations of the publisher. For some writ-ers, this leads back, in a kind of awful circle, to writer's block. How can I write a book that will be as well re-ceived as my last one? How can I ever earn out an ad-vance that large? This story I'm working on now, is it going to be a letdown to the fans who love me? Fearing to disappoint, and bowing to pressures from publisher and agent, some writers produce a slightly varied version of the same bestseller over and over again until the reading public cries, "Enough!" And the writer's spirit shrivels.

On a more modest level, there are authors who have a book or a few books published and can't seem to talk about anything else. Because their work has received some acclaim — often after years of labor — they become absorbed in their own melodrama to the point where the illness of a friend's mother, or the concerns of their spouse, or the non-literary ambitions of a nephew pale in comparison. This can be especially dangerous for one who teaches, because in that situation a classroom full of students is required to hang on your every word. When you give a reading, people listen attentively for 40 minutes and then spend another half hour asking questions. Afterwards, they hand you compliments and buy your book. What sometimes happens is that the writer carries that relationship over into other areas of life and begins to want to be the center of attention all the time, to have everyone listening to his or her pearls of wisdom.

Sometimes, the need to earn money was what drove the author to work so hard, and once that need has been met, once the bills are being paid without so much trouble, the drive to write evaporates. Many of us would not be devastated by this scenario.

Success is a good thing, of course. Most writers I know handle it well. Some of my very successful friends are incredibly generous with their time, advice, and money. After his novel, *Cry The Beloved Country*, became an international bestseller, the South African author Alan Paton received hundreds of thousands of pieces of mail from around the world, and answered all of them personally.

It may not be necessary to go to that extent of generosity, but when success comes, it is nice to remember those who helped you get there — from friends and a supportive spouse, to early readers, mentors, teachers, librarians, agents, editors, publicists, and those fine people who lay down cash for your books.

Demon Fifteen
Always Taking

Before or after success comes, it is wise to be aware of what I call the Demon of Taking. In some people the desperate urge to achieve writing success breeds an attitude of the most intense narcissism. These are people who want desperately to have a published book, but spend very little money buying books that others have written. These are people who seem willing not only to make the healthy sacrifices necessary to build a writing career, but also to make the unnecessary, unattractive, unethical ones. In a workshop, they will try to monopolize the teacher's time and attention, as if the other students there, who have worked as hard and paid a similar tuition, do not exist.

Writers who have had some success might try to climb farther up the literary ladder on the backs of family members and friends, using the travails of those people as material for books, in spite of the fact that the public display of their frailties will cause them pain. Or, writing a review, the somewhat successful author will trample on the work of another writer in a way he would have found intolerable and inexcusable had it been done to him.

These days, when the marketing of a book sometimes

seems a more important element of its success than the actual quality of the writing, and when publishers have smaller and smaller budgets for publicity, some authors turn into heedless self-promoters. They have not been in touch with a friend for years, but then send that friend a note asking her to buy their new book and spread the word. In casual conversation, some authors are so wrapped up in their own melodrama that all they can talk about is their work, their reviews, their struggle, their new idea for a title, their fan mail, even their failures . . . as if the other writer, standing a few feet away, has been turned into one enormous ear.

I think we all have some of these tendencies. Every writer I know, everyone who even thinks about writing something for someone else to read, has a degree of narcissism and egotism in him. Maybe it's true to say that every human being has some of that, fixated as we are more on our own problems and joys than on anyone else's. Maybe the impulse to have a love relationship, to bear and raise children, or to teach, help, or advise, is nature's way of breaking us out of this cage of self-concern. As with the other demons, the important thing is to be aware of these tendencies, to struggle to see them clearly. Almost always, with a slight twist, a demon can be turned into a friend. We can learn to take and enjoy our share, and, at the same time, allow others to have theirs.

Sixteen
Where The Demons Are Conquered

Obviously enough, the field on which the demons do battle with our creative energies is the field of the mind. And yet, it seems to me sometimes that writers fail to nurture and cultivate that soil in a way that reflects a sincere commitment to our work. We place so much emphasis on technique, as if what matters is the hoe and rake and pitchfork and rototiller, and not the dirt in which the seed is planted.

Modern society is continually offering us opportunities to litter, clutter, pollute and poison the field of the mind. We fill it with a thousand errands and responsibilities, a million superficial entertainments. Just as the serious student of writing has to carve out some sacred time in which to create and revise, he or she also has to fence off a protected space — one calm, untroubled area into which ideas are free to fall and take root, like seeds carried on the wind. So many people come up to me at talks and workshops and ask, "Where do your ideas come from?" and "How do you focus on a long project?" and "How do you discipline yourself to work when there is nothing and no one forcing you, or organizing things for you?" "How

have you been able to publish so many books?" The answer to all of these questions has to do with fencing off,
cultivating, and giving plenty of water and sunlight to that
part of the mind where writing sprouts and flourishes. I
know very well that I am not the most talented, energetic,
or ambitious writer on earth. But, over the course of thirty years, I have learned how to maintain this quiet space
for myself, and how to work efficiently there, and I have
made a career that suits me.

To some extent, all writers know how to protect and
use this space, otherwise they would never have been published. But I think many teachers of writing are afraid to
talk about this part of the process for fear of sounding like
a preacher trying to convert, or a pseudo-psychologist
without the appropriate training. There is, of course, a
risk in these kinds of discussions. Writing is a personal
occupation, and the mind is a tender place where outsid-
ers' fingers are not usually welcome. But it's a shame, I
think, even a dereliction of duty, for teachers of writing
not to put the correct emphasis on this interior dimension.
It is not our business, of course, to tell someone else how
to think or live. And yet writing, more so than other areas
of study, is intimately connected to the process of thinking, and so it would seem perfectly natural — in addition
to talking about the best ways to build a character or set a
scene — to talk about caring for the place where those
characters and scenes originate.

At least part of the creative urge is buried in the subconscious. In order to write something in a way that

reaches other people, we have to bring those thoughts, stories, and ideas "up" through the conscious mind and put them into an external form that makes sense to others. Readers absorb them through their own conscious minds, but, I believe, the power of the best work echoes down into their subconscious, and that echo is our real link with other human beings. A story moves someone because it is our mystery speaking to their mystery via the code of language. A work of non-fiction, whether an article, personal essay or a book, provokes, enlightens or educates via this same process, this ineffable link, this baffling power of letters on a page or screen.

To leave the earlier agricultural metaphor behind for a moment, I sometimes think of this process as being similar to finding water beneath the earth, or tuning into a radio station. In order to get the well water into our home, we have to know where to dig and drill and then we have to keep the pipe clear of debris. In order to get a radio signal we have to go to certain strong frequencies on the dial.

The same is true for inspiration. How can we expect to have ideas come to us if the mind is cluttered with errands, duties, worries, plans, and a myriad of pleasurable distractions? And yet, teachers of writing rarely talk about ways of uncluttering the field, keeping the well pipe clear, or tuning, at will, to the frequency on which our subconscious operates. It's too vague, too amorphous, too easy to mock. It's so much simpler and less risky to talk about sentence structure and pacing, simile and point of view.

Writers who can be productive, who can slay the demons of writer's block, perfectionism or false confidence,
are often the writers who have found a way to keep the
field of the mind — at least one part of it — clear of noise
and debris. There are numerous ways of doing this. In
years past, especially, many writers and other artists were
thought to depend on drink or drugs to help their minds
float away from the mess of daily living. I've found,
among students especially, that the romantic image of the
stricken artist, suffering for his or her work and taking refuge in drink or drugs, is a hard one to dismiss. There is a
seductive melodrama to all that — the brave, lonely, usually impoverished creative soul engaged in a terrible struggle
to make art.

Maybe. In some cases. Countering that, however, is a
vast array of creative geniuses who seem to have been able
to sink a clean pipe down into the aquifer of the subconscious without having to light a not so clean pipe of hash-
ish. There is a long list of well adjusted, even happy writers
to set against others who wrestled with depression and addiction, and whose misery eventually resulted in suicide by
one form or another. As alluring as the creative life is, and
as much as I love it, I would find abject misery and addiction a very high price to pay for the privilege of expressing
myself on the page.

This is not to say that anyone — creative or otherwise
— chooses to be depressed or to live in anguish. We are
all made differently, we all suffer in various ways, we pay
various kinds of prices for the gift of being alive, and I

don't think it's wise to cast judgments on others' struggles.

I do believe, though, that the romantic image of the miserable artist may be giving way, in modern times, to a wider spectrum of possibility for creative types. And I do believe it is important to make an effort to nurture the mind the way an athlete would nurture the body. If you are training for the Olympics, you take some care about how you treat your body — what you eat, what exercise you do, what kind of activities you pursue or avoid. Why shouldn't we, in training for the task of writing, pay equal attention to the mind?

The methods for cultivating a clear mind are as varied as the individual personality. For me, almost every writing day has to have a period of physical activity and a period of contemplation. I've had a meditation practice for thirty years, and usually do one session of at least 30 minutes a day; in the afternoons I'll leave the desk and mow the lawn, play golf, practice karate or yoga, walk our country road, take a swim with my kids. The point is to have some kind of practice that is aimed at sweeping away the interior rubble so that the seeds can have space to grow. For some, this means a religious practice — prayer, regular services, meditation (though meditation need not be linked to any particular religious path). For others it is regular exercise, time in nature, gardening, a walk with a pet, travel, music, painting, knitting, a quiet cup of tea out on the deck. It is important — I would even say essential — to have something along these lines, some regular refuge, and important that it serves to clear away the debris and not add to the clutter. Just as writers have their rituals — a certain kind of pen or paper, a period of settling activities — it is useful, I think, to spend some time, as Michael Miller puts it, "letting the well fill up." Maybe it is helpful if this activity is something wordless. Athletes often speak about going beyond their thoughts. Certainly that is an aspect of meditation. Often, we do things we enjoy — taking a swim in the ocean, playing with a pet, listening to music — precisely, if unintentionally, because these activities allow the word-making part of the mind to take time off.

Just as I believe there should be no etched-in-stone rules having to do with the technical aspects of writing — no "you must always" or "you should never", I also believe that this advice about a physical or non-literary practice does not apply to everyone. I have sports-averse friends who are perfectly happy reading and writing for every waking hour, taking time off only to eat and bathe.

But I recently spoke with a teacher who had great success when she started making her students meditate for a few minutes in class before writing an assignment. I know how helpful a long walk can be for me if I am struggling with a scene or the ending of a book. I believe that Hemingway's life captured our imaginations in part because of its emphasis on the physical — hiking, skiing, hunting, boxing, time in nature. In at least one interview, Robert Stone talked about taking his dog for a walk in the woods before a day of work. Vonnegut smoked cigarettes. Francis Mayes, author of *Under the Tuscan Sun*, seemed to take great inspiration from home repair projects and plying the markets for groceries. John Updike played golf. John Irving wrestled. Craig Nova rows a single scull. Tracy Kidder works out at the health club and goes fishing in the Florida Keys.

I think it's easy to read about these "practices" and not connect them to the process of clearing the mind. Probably, many of the writers who have this kind of routine do not think of it as a practice, an exercise to unclutter the field. But it seems obvious to me that that's what it is. We study the technical aspects of their work; we are fascinated with their schedules and quirks, with their personal dramas. Maybe it is wise to pay some attention to this other dimension of the creative life, too, and give ourselves an advantage in the battles we must wage against the demons that keep us from writing. Those demons are real. The damage they do is difficult to measure because it is contained in the absence of work, and in the invisible realm of the author's scarred spirit. I am intimately familiar with this damage and with many of the demons that cause it, and I have put together this small book in the sincere hope that it will help other writers, at all levels, in the ongoing battle to set their truth and vision onto the page.

Made in the USA
Middletown, DE
23 November 2019

79294342R00083